Early Praise for *Designing Data Governance From the Ground Up*

This book is an immediately actionable resource for any team working to build out a data governance plan. Maffeo's smart and thorough advice is applicable across organizations, whether in industry or the non-profit sector. Using this book as a guide, leaders and stakeholders can execute on a strategy right away.

➤ **Lisa Tagliaferri, PhD**
Researcher, Educator, and Software Developer

Many organizations make the mistake of going deep on technology before understanding the foundational components needed for a robust data governance program. Maffeo distills the most important aspects of data governance into a clear set of fundamental building blocks all organizations can use to improve visibility and control. Whether you're just starting your data governance journey or are in the process of re-structuring and optimizing an existing program, put Lauren Maffeo's *Designing Data Governance* at the top of your reading list.

➤ **Diana Kelley**
Co-Founder, SecurityCurve

Lauren Maffeo has written a brilliant and must-read masterclass on building an outstanding data-driven culture that takes all organizations to the highest level of data governance. Read this comprehensive and crystal-clear guide to collecting, securing and managing your organization's data. Learn from one of the best.

➤ **Kweku Opoku-Agyemang, Ph.D.**
CEO, Machine Learning X Doing

A simple and easy to comprehend guide to build fundamental blocks of your data governance program.

➤ **Gaurav Patole**
Global Data Governance Senior Manager, BGC

As part of my legal practice, I have spent a lot of time researching and curating a list of my favorite articles and books addressing developments in AI, privacy, and data governance. *Designing Data Governance* is among my favorite books on this topic. Lauren Maffeo tackles this challenging subject matter effortlessly answering the "how to and why" questions about implementing a data governance program in easy-to-read language. I recommend this book to anyone who wants to learn more about data governance generally and those who are tackling data governance implementation for the first time. I'll add that this book is particularly timely given the increased regulatory focus on privacy, data security, and companies' use of data.

➤ **Tamra Moore**
Partner, King & Spalding LLP

Designing Data Governance from the Ground Up
Six Steps to Build a Data-Driven Culture

Lauren Maffeo

The Pragmatic Bookshelf

Raleigh, North Carolina

Many of the designations used by manufacturers and sellers to distinguish their products are claimed as trademarks. Where those designations appear in this book, and The Pragmatic Programmers, LLC was aware of a trademark claim, the designations have been printed in initial capital letters or in all capitals. The Pragmatic Starter Kit, The Pragmatic Programmer, Pragmatic Programming, Pragmatic Bookshelf, PragProg and the linking *g* device are trademarks of The Pragmatic Programmers, LLC.

Every precaution was taken in the preparation of this book. However, the publisher assumes no responsibility for errors or omissions, or for damages that may result from the use of information (including program listings) contained herein.

For our complete catalog of hands-on, practical, and Pragmatic content for software developers, please visit *https://pragprog.com*.

The team that produced this book includes:

CEO: Dave Rankin
COO: Janet Furlow
Managing Editor: Tammy Coron
Development Editor: Brian P. Hogan
Copy Editor: Karen Galle
Layout: Gilson Graphics
Founders: Andy Hunt and Dave Thomas

For sales, volume licensing, and support, please contact *support@pragprog.com*.

For international rights, please contact *rights@pragprog.com*.

ISBN-13: 978-1-68050-980-9
Book version: P1.0—January 2023

Contents

Acknowledgments

I once read a newsletter by Katie Hawkins-Gaar in which she said that when starting a new book, she always flips to the acknowledgments first. It tells her who the book's author is, what they value, and how they thank the people who helped them meet their goals. "A novel may have just one author's name on the cover, but it took an entire crew of people to make that book happen," she writes. "When you think about it, most things are that way. We rarely do anything alone."

It's ironic how lonely the book-writing process can feel when each author has a team behind them. The last few years showed me how much help we all need in this ever-changing world. I would be remiss not to thank those who helped me bring this book to life.

An author's work lives and dies by their editor. Brian Hogan, you struck the right chord of pushing me to do more and encouraging me to step back as needed. There were several times throughout my writing process when I doubted my ability to finish. I finished because of your advocacy for this book and your belief that the world needs it. Thank you; I will miss working with you.

Writing a book in Markdown was one of my most humbling career moments. Tammy Coron, you have a sense of patience that I hope I'll gain someday. You took calls on a whim to walk me through each question, and you never wavered in your willingness to help. When I couldn't see a path forward, you always threw me a much-needed lifeline.

To my techical reviewers who read this book's first draft, you gave me the courage to bring this book into the world. Your feedback helped me view it through fresh eyes, see what I had missed, and strengthen its resolve. Your own wisdom is woven throughout each chapter. Thank you Jason Block, Jason Browning, Joe Comeau, Ben Cotton, Victoria Guido, Willem Koenders, Brian Parady, Donna Sawyer, and Lisa Tagliaferri.

Taryn, I can't tell you how touching your excitement for me and this book has been. You walked me out of the woods when I felt lost and have been my cheerleader, from signing my book contract to publishing the final draft. My friendship with you is one of the greatest gifts I'll ever get.

Jenelle, I'll never forget the tears of joy in your eyes when I told you I had gotten a book contract. I didn't expect friends and family to care about this book as much as I did. Your enthusiasm proved me wrong.

Ella and Luce, you kept me company during my often-lonely bookwriting process. From sleeping at my feet while I wrote at dawn to crashing my conference calls, your presence put me at ease and reminded me to take much-needed walk breaks!

Mom and Dad, you're a foundation of unconditional love. You've always given me the grace to make my own decisions and mistakes, which I felt free to do because I knew our bond would endure. You are the most important people in my life.

Preface

I don't need to tell you how essential data is. If you picked up this book, then you already know that data powers today's most profitable businesses. With companies like Google and Meta boasting data-based business models, it's no surprise that 99 percent of firms said they planned to invest in AI and data in 2021.[1]

While data can bring incredible value, most businesses haven't unlocked it yet. Poor data quality costs businesses millions per year, with some paying close to a quarter of their annual revenue.[2] If that's not enough of a reason to change, consider the cultural impact of bad data.

A 2021 survey of C-suite executives found that while investments in AI and big data keep rising, the number of respondents who say they're data-driven declined. Just one in four respondents said they thought their organization was data-driven, down from 37.8 percent the year before.[3] Those surveyed consistently cited cultural hardships as a far bigger blocker than technical limitations. Employee skills gaps, outdated business processes, resistance to change, and poor choice of tools add up over time. If you've wondered why just 13 percent of machine learning models make it to production, there's no shortage of culprits.

I've seen this firsthand in my own work. I spent several years researching AI techniques as an analyst at Gartner. My job was to advise clients on the latest technical trends that could help them grow their businesses. I quickly realized that even if most of these businesses started using AI tomorrow, their efforts would be futile. Most businesses had such low data maturity that they weren't ready to harness technology like machine learning.

---

1. https://c6abb8db-514c-4f5b-b5a1-fc710f1e464e.filesusr.com/ugd/e5361a_76709448ddc6490981f0cbea42d51508.pdf
2. https://sloanreview.mit.edu/article/seizing-opportunity-in-data-quality/
3. https://hbr.org/2021/02/why-is-it-so-hard-to-become-a-data-driven-company

When I started working on a technical team, I saw how even organizations that exist to disseminate data are not immune to governance problems. I've seen clients possess millions of unique data points and several centuries' worth of datasets. They also lacked any documentation showing which servers this data lived on, how these servers integrated with each other, and the workflows that shared this data with their users. As a result, their data dissemination processes were not streamlined, took days to complete, and involved several people per release, with no automation involved.

It doesn't have to be this way. Consider the efforts involved in bringing a new product to market. You would write a go-to-market plan with a high-level strategy for how you want the product to help users. You would work with colleagues across sales, marketing, engineering, and customer success to collect intel that will help you build this product. You would write a roadmap showing the key tasks and milestones each stakeholder must meet to bring this product to the right customers at the right time. Then, you would keep governing this product throughout its life cycle.

Your data strategy deserves no less attention than your product strategy. The good news is, a lot of techniques needed to build great products apply to data governance as well. Mastering the basics—finding a framework, selecting data stewards, building your data governance council, and writing a roadmap—helps you take your data projects to the next stage of maturity.

This book is your blueprint to bring data projects past production. By building and executing a plan to use data for decision-making, you'll gain the first six steps you need to build a data governance plan that improves business outcomes and engages colleagues. By putting this into practice, you'll build trust, increase cooperation, and improve efficiency when it comes to using data. My goal is for you to start reading this book on your flight from Los Angeles and land in New York with the steps you need to start building a data governance plan tomorrow.

Is This Book for Me?

I wrote this book for decision-makers in medium-to-large organizations (100+ employees), especially those working in highly regulated industries where data governance is legally required. I believe that all organizations should practice data governance, regardless of size or industry. It's easier to build programs from scratch than to incur the technical debt involved in fixing broken practices. That said, you will gain the most from this book if you already work in an organization that has the staff numbers needed to execute governance. While you don't need an enormous team, you can't do all of this work alone.

I wrote this book for readers who know they need help leveraging their data, but are not sure how to get governance off the ground. It's for readers who hold decision-making power at their organizations, and are tasked with finding solutions for business problems. If the CEO of your accounting firm wants advice on how to take your robotic process automation project past production, or your higher education client's asking how to manage metadata, this book will make the case for you.

That reader definition is intentionally broad. It's true that I wrote this book for senior leaders in business and tech roles to help them build blueprints for data governance. But if a junior data engineer or mid-level manager finishes this book without learning how to harness data in their organizations—and how to engage colleagues in this effort—I don't think I've done my job. In today's organizations, there's no role that data doesn't impact. You might not be an engineer or CTO, but we need you to succeed just the same.

That's especially true if you work in a highly regulated industry like finance, education, or healthcare. While all organizations must use data responsibly, global standards demand that some sectors practice more data discretion. You'll find this book especially helpful if you work in a sector that's controlled by a range of governance rules. Data protections differ widely around the world. If your organization wants to serve a global market, your data governance must meet global standards.

Finally, if you're a student enrolled in a data science or analytics program, I hope this book will help you walk into your next role with the confidence to lead crucial conversations. I once spoke at a data science conference which touched on some of the principles we'll cover in this book. When I asked attendees with Data Science Master's degrees how much instruction they got on data governance, they all said, "None."

They had attended top academic programs and earned data science roles at attractive companies once they graduated. Yet the more I spoke with them, the more I heard how they were expected to do all things data without the knowledge they needed to drive substantial change. These conversations taught me that data science is now too big a burden for one colleague to carry. Without help from the whole organization, today's data scientists will collapse under its weight.

Now that I've told you whom this book is for, it's worth mentioning what's absent. We won't debate what data science is, discuss data training techniques like linear regression, or explain how to do ensemble modeling, because that knowledge exists elsewhere. I wrote this book because you can throw a proverbial stone online and hit a blog post about data science, but results for data governance searches are scarce. This book fills the void I found when I searched for data governance resources that I could use in my own work. I wrote the book I wished I'd had, based on knowledge I learned the hard way.

I'll reference technical tools and methods where applicable, like Hadoop software utilities and two-factor authentication. The last two chapters are more technical than the first four; they'll cover how to practice data governance once your project is in development and production environments. You'll gain the most value from this book if you're familiar with these concepts. That said, you shouldn't need to hold a traditionally technical role (like data engineer or front-end developer) to learn something from these chapters and this book. If you're a designer, program manager, or quality assurance engineer working on data projects, I hope you'll bring this book's knowledge back to your teams.

What's in This Book?

When you finish this book, you'll have the first six steps you'll need to build a data governance plan that aligns your efforts to clean, collect, and secure the data you'll need to power pipelines. Here's what you'll find in each chapter:

Chapter 1: Find Your Data Framework

How will your organization control data access, implement new regulatory policies, and track activity for data models? If you lack answers to any of these questions, it's time for a data governance framework. This chapter will show you how to use one, and write a mission statement for data use to guide your work through the rest of this book.

Chapter 2: Select Data Stewards

Data governance isn't one sole person or team's job. This chapter will share how to find the best data stewards in your business to own specific types of data and metadata so that data governance is truly a team effort.

Chapter 3: Build Your Data Governance Council

Data stewards can't collaborate if they stay in silos. Chapter 3 shares how to create and manage a data governance council that keeps colleagues engaged for the long haul.

Chapter 4: Write Your Data Roadmap

Roadmaps build business-wide consensus for how to use data, approve tools, prioritize projects, and more. This chapter will show you how to write a roadmap for your data governance work.

Chapter 5: Practice Governance-Driven Development

Data governance is futile if it doesn't improve your development work. Using a case study from Netflix, you will learn how to embed data governance principles into your data projects.

Chapter 6: Monitor Data in Production

Data governance doesn't stop once your models reach production. This chapter shares the steps your stewards must take to keep data's quality and security aligned with your governance standards.

How Will This Book Help Me Reach My Goals?

This book shows you how to build a foundation for collecting, securing, and managing your organization's data. You can't progress your data projects without doing some essential groundwork first.

Establishing data governance that's strategic, follows a framework, engages stewards, and uses a roadmap is hard work. It takes time, resources, and company-wide buy-in. This book will show you how to do it right the first time and set yourself up for long-term success.

CHAPTER 1

Find Your Data Framework

Frameworks are like the foundation of your house. If your house is not built on a strong structure that can withstand storms, the whole house will collapse. That's why you must use a framework to design data governance; it's the building block of successful data projects. If you've never used a data framework before, you don't need to reinvent the wheel. You can use existing frameworks to help guide your efforts. The key is knowing your organization well enough to apply a data framework that will help them meet their goals.

This chapter will show you how to define why your business exists and how each data project will fulfill the business mission. From there, you'll connect that mission statement to a data framework that addresses core aspects of data governance, from transparency and ethics to trust and security. When you're done, you'll have a blueprint to manage all your business data from the top down, rather than feeling overwhelmed by doing it piecemeal.

Define Data Governance

Before you select a data governance framework, go more granular and define data governance. It's an admittedly nebulous term that can seem to mean everything and nothing. Depending on your background, business, and a range of other factors, data governance can seem academic or irrelevant, even if you work in a data-focused role.

Data governance is a multidisciplinary approach to making and upholding standards that manage data at scale. It helps organizations assess data sourcing, quality, and security at all stages of the data pipeline, from receiving the first spreadsheets with raw data to monitoring that data's quality once it's in production.

Data governance engages employees across organizations to co-create the standards, techniques, and metrics that measure success. This is perhaps the most crucial aspect of strong data governance: bringing data management beyond your IT and DevSecOps teams. By building a data governance council comprised of data stewards that own aspects of your data framework, you give a sense of shared ownership for data that transcends roles. You'll learn how to do this in the next few chapters.

Strong data governance teams do deep, foundational work before diving headfirst into data projects. Each team member knows why they're pursuing each project, which training techniques they'll use, how they procure data, and which metrics they'll use. In short, they have a strategy for why and how they want to use data, guided by a roadmap to help them hit key benchmarks. But this strategy doesn't start with data; it goes higher up to the heart of your business.

Most data-based initiatives fail when leaders don't invest in choosing success metrics, selecting data stewards, starting with small-scale projects, and doing data quality assurance. You can't do any of these things if you don't know why your business exists, or how you want data to help achieve your business goals.

Investing in the "Why?" of data governance early yields long-term success when it's time to tackle more ambitious projects. I learned early in my career that when companies made these investments, it didn't take long for them to start seeing returns. Those investments start by completing a few key tasks.

Clarify Your Company's Mission Statement

When I was a research analyst at Gartner, I surveyed several hundred employees at North American businesses with 500 or fewer employees. I wanted to learn how they used data to make business decisions and how confident (or not) they were in doing so. I also wanted to know if having tools and colleagues devoted to data increased employee confidence in using this data to make business decisions.

Across the sectors surveyed, I found the following facts:

- Employing data scientists makes business leaders more confident that they have the right data and insights to make business decisions.

- Companies with full-time employees who analyze data also use business intelligence (BI) software more often.

- Business leaders that use BI software rate the data-based decisions they make as more impactful.

- A positive correlation exists between how confident people are in their data decision-making and how important they believe data is to their businesses.

Two things struck me as I reviewed these results. The first is that investing in tools and employees to govern data improves business outcomes. The businesses that feel most comfortable with data are the same ones that create roles devoted to governing it. They also invest in software and other data science tools to help employees govern said data.

That said, it is equally important for businesses to decentralize their data. This involves giving each team leader, even those in non-technical roles, the autonomy to own data within their domain. Whether you manage a sales team or a hospital, leaders across all lines of business should be empowered to boost their teams' outcomes using data. It helps everyone contribute to the bigger business picture.

If you aim to achieve these outcomes, you'll need to do some foundational work first, and that work doesn't start with data. To use data effectively, start by clarifying why your business exists. Put another way, ask yourself this question:

"What's my company's mission statement?"

I know what you're thinking: "Isn't it obvious what my company does? Why do I need to bother writing it down, let alone writing a mission statement?"

Here's the thing: you likely do know what your business does on a daily basis. Hopefully, you know how your own role fulfills that work as well. If you're a CTO, that means you manage the purchase decisions and rollouts of all tech across your organization. On any given day, you assess security risks, report updates to stakeholders, and research ways to improve your company's IT.

Now, ask yourself why these daily tasks are part of your job. As CTO, you're responsible for managing all aspects of your company's technology. Your mission is to ensure that all the technology your company uses and deploys, internally and externally, advances company goals. If you're unsure whether a specific technology or strategy helps achieve these goals, it's time to revisit your company's mission. How can you ensure that you're making the right decisions without knowing what your business's north star is?

This might sound like a philosophical exercise that you can't spare time for. Time and money constraints can prevent senior leaders from asking these questions as often as they should. But without knowing the answers to these questions, you can't affect meaningful change in your role. Likewise, without knowing why your business wants to invest in data projects, you won't write a successful plan to govern data over the long term. You can't use data to grow revenue, improve products, increase customer satisfaction scores, or lower supply chain costs without knowing how data impacts your company's mission. And if you can't explain why you want to invest resources in data efforts, you'll waste time and money that could be spent elsewhere.

So, the first step on your path to using data is to ensure that you know your company's mission statement. If you are unsure what your organization's mission statement is, this is your cue to ask senior leadership. You are searching for a single sentence that captures why your company exists, and how its existence adds value to the world. If you look up some of the world's most famous brands, you'll find succinct statements of purpose:

- Warby Parker: "To offer designer eyewear at a revolutionary price, while leading the way for socially conscious businesses."

- Workday: "To put people at the center of enterprise software."

- Tesla: "To accelerate the world's transition to sustainable energy."

- TED: "Spread ideas."

- Invisible Children: "To end violence and exploitation facing our world's most isolated and vulnerable communities."

These brands have clear reasons for existing. They know the unique value they bring and what they aim to offer the world. If these famous brands are also exceptional companies, they ensure that every team member knows why they exist, and how these mission statements drive each colleague's daily work. If TED's Head of Product knows that the brand's mission is to spread ideas, they'll approach their product management work through that lens.

Now, it's time to take the mission statement concept one step further. Let's review Warby Parker's mission statement through a data-focused lens:

- How might Warby Parker use data to offer designer eyewear at a revolutionary price?

- What data would they need to achieve this goal?

- Why do they need this specific data to achieve their mission?

- Who would collect, clean, and manage this data?

- Where would these colleagues store the data? An on-premise server? An Amazon Web Services (AWS) environment? Neither?

With those questions in mind, apply the same data-focused lens to your own company's mission statement. This clarity will help you answer a crucial question: "What's the point of using data at all?"

To write a mission statement for data, clarify how you want data to enhance your business in one or two written sentences. The more specific you can be, the better. It's not enough to say, "Our company will give all teams the tools and training they need to make data-based decisions."

Instead, try something like this:

"Our organization will enable all team leads to access data within [BI/analytics software of choice, like Tableau]. This will empower everyone to achieve our shared business goal of increasing customer satisfaction scores by 10 percent by 2025."

Once you've drafted your data's mission statement, you'll use a data governance framework to execute that mission.

Find Your Data Governance Framework

Think of data governance frameworks like you would software frameworks. Software provides functionality for all, while frameworks make that software specific to diverse applications. Data provides information, while frameworks help you manage that data in unique business contexts.

Data on its own has minimal value if you don't know how or why you want to use it. For instance, let's say that your digital marketing director gives your data scientists a set of statistics about user behavior on your company website. Your data science team wants to build an algorithm predicting which user demographics are more likely to buy certain products, and which webpages each user segment will most likely visit. Before your data science team can achieve this goal, they'll need to answer several questions:

- Which data sources does the marketing team use? Did they collect this data from Siteimprove? Google Analytics? A secondary source, like a contractor?

- Which format is this data in? Will your data scientists need to convert the format before they're able to use the data?

- Did someone on the marketing team clean this dataset? Are there duplicates, incorrect labels, and so on? There's a reason why some estimates say that 80 percent of data science is cleaning spreadsheets:[1] if you feed an algorithm bad data, you can't expect great results.

- Does the marketing team "own" this dataset, its quality, and decisions about how this data is used? If not, is this the data science team's responsibility? The answer itself matters less than having one. Regardless of what you want to do with this data, someone must be responsible for it.

In this scenario, data is the statistics which share information about user behavior. A governance framework helps your team apply that data in an accountable, business-specific context. Since frameworks are support structures to build upon, your colleagues in this example situation have the highest chance of success if they do the marketing-to-data-science handoff with a framework in mind.

You do not have to reinvent the wheel when it comes to using a data governance framework; several frameworks already exist. Gartner's data governance framework[2] is especially helpful because it covers the key areas your data governance efforts will need to address:

- Values and outcomes
- Trust
- Accountability and decision rights
- Transparency and ethics
- Risk and security
- Education and training
- Collaboration and culture

You'll learn how to implement these sections in future chapters. For now, let's review each section in more detail to see how they all enhance your mission statement.

Values and Outcomes

Without clear metrics, rationale, and conversations about how to use data, your colleagues won't see how it applies to their daily tasks. They are more likely to infer that you're putting more work on their already full plates.

To avoid this, center all conversations about data on both your business mission statement and your mission statement for using data. When someone in your organization proposes a new machine learning operations (MLOps) project, map it back to your organization's business values, priorities, and

---

1. https://hbr.org/2018/08/what-data-scientists-really-do-according-to-35-data-scientists
2. https://www.gartner.com/smarterwithgartner/7-key-foundations-for-modern-data-and-analytics-governance

processes. Likewise, when you write down metrics for success using data, make sure you attribute each metric to a certain colleague, and that those colleagues are bought in.

Sound overwhelming? It doesn't have to be. Start with one data project before trying to do too much at once. Use it as a model for additional projects by taking the following steps:

- Map the project back to your business mission statement. (Again, why are you doing this? You shouldn't prioritize flashy new efforts without a clear reason for doing so.)

- Write a mission statement for using data in this project, including success metrics to gauge how well you fulfilled that statement.

- Pick metrics to measure based on your most pressing business problems (decreasing the length of a task's duration, increasing the number of user logins, and so on).

- Keep the project's stakeholders informed before, during, and after development.

- Meet regularly (at least weekly) to track project progress and highlight value-adds/blockers.

Your data governance councilmembers will fulfill these tasks to keep each data project aligned with bigger business objectives. The next two chapters will cover the role data stewards play in fulfilling this work, and how to build a data governance council that measures value-based outcomes per project.

Trust

Trust is the backbone of any strategy, especially when dealing with data. You already know that owning lots of data is not valuable unless you manage and use it strategically. The full picture is even less rosy. Left ungoverned, having lots of data is a liability that can decrease trust not just in your data, but in your business writ large.

A 2021 survey analysis by the Bank for International Settlements (BIS)[3] revealed that Americans have several concerns about how various sectors use their personal data. The COVID-19 pandemic made Americans even less willing to share personal data with a range of actors, from big tech firms (the least trusted sector) to local governments. When asked which risks they're

---

3. https://www.bis.org/publ/bisbull42.pdf

especially scared of, identity theft ranked highest, followed by data abuse and risk to personal safety.

That's why your data framework must advance trust in two distinct ways: maximizing data's value while minimizing its harm. Everything else you do, from recruiting colleagues for your data governance council to setting security standards, should roll back up to those key goals.

Accountability and Decision Rights

Once you know that your data framework must build trust, the next step is to confirm which people will make each decision about data. This task requires you to engage colleagues across your business. So, as you review each step of this framework, consider which colleagues are most qualified to own them.

You'll want to include colleagues across the organization in your plan to use data and make decisions about it. That's how you will build your data stewardship team, which you'll explore in the next chapter.

Questions about data accountability and decision rights should answer some key questions: Who owns data within each respective domain? Which team or person is responsible for it, and who decides which teams or people gain access to it?

For example, your sales director might manage your organization's data about sales leads using software like Salesforce. In this case, the sales director owns data in the sales domain and makes decisions about how it's accessed. If anyone else in the organization needs to view leads data, they should feel confident requesting it from your sales director.

Transparency and Ethics

"Values and ethics are not a whole separate endeavor...the very activity of data cleaning is inherently an act that requires one to make ethical, moral, and normative choices."

I found that quote in a tweet from Adeba Birhane, a Cognitive Science PhD candidate at the University College Dublin Complex Software Lab. Years later, I haven't seen a more accurate assessment for why ethics lie at the heart of data work. Each aspect of this work, from collecting and cleaning data to which training techniques you use for algorithms, reinforces your organization's values. So, waiting to discuss data ethics in your team retrospectives is unethical in itself.

The well-documented consequences of algorithmic bias affect—and, in some cases, ruin[4]—users' lives. Our colleagues in law, medicine, and other influential sectors take oaths pledging to do no harm. We must pledge to do the same with data.

Like governance itself, too many people still consider data ethics a standalone project that leaders will "get to" when convenient. The reality couldn't be further from the truth. Ethics, and transparency about how your team makes data-based decisions, must lie at the center of your data governance. That's because there is no trust without transparency.

To show customers that you have their best interests at heart, you'll need a clear rationale for how and why your organization collects, cleans, organizes, and presents data. You can make a lot of headway with a code of data ethics that is:

- Clear
- Defensible
- Documented

Any data ethics code must align with your respective company and data mission statements. It should also explain who is responsible for making which decisions about data. You'll see throughout this book how each part of this framework intersects with others. By assigning accountability and prioritizing trust, you prove that your business integrates ethics into your data work and is transparent about how you make data-based decisions.

Risk and Security

Ungoverned data yields a range of security risks. As of October 2021, The Identity Theft Research Center (ITRC)[5] reported a 17 percent increase in data breaches over 2020. Many of those breaches ruined supply chains, like DarkSide's ransomware attack on Colonial Pipeline that yielded gas shortages up the eastern U.S. seaboard.

Keeping your data safe and secure involves being risk-aware via data governance. You don't want to be a brand that's known for making mea culpas due to data mismanagement. While you can't prevent every possible problem, you can avoid potential problems, or at least ease them, if you govern data with a risk-aware approach.

---

4. https://www.brookings.edu/research/police-surveillance-and-facial-recognition-why-data-privacy-is-an-imperative-for-communities-of-color/
5. https://fortune.com/2021/10/06/data-breach-2021-2020-total-hacks/

Having a multistep framework like this, led by a cross-departmental team, is the first step to staying risk-aware. It decreases risk by boosting transparency across teams. It also gives team leads the chance to evaluate their data use against the organization's mission statement and helps you integrate your organization's enterprise information security framework into one environment.

Education and Training

Implementing data governance involves new, unfamiliar policies and standards. To roll out data governance the right way, you'll need to provide training and development resources to all your data stewards. This will teach them what success looks like and equip them to co-lead data governance.

Working with HR will help you build a long-term training plan for data stewards in business and technical roles. This has the added bonus of allowing you to weave data stewardship goals into each steward's role description and employee evaluations.

This is crucial since you'll want to give credit to the work each steward achieves helping your business meet its objectives. If stewards know that they'll earn formal recognition for their efforts, they'll be more inclined to help.

Collaboration and Culture

You already know that leaders across the organization should be involved in data governance decisions. The trick is to make governance more than a compliance check. If your organization views governance work as bureaucratic, or as additional work beyond their daily roles, you'll have a much tougher time getting buy-in. To succeed in having sustained impact, data governance should take the form of knowledge sharing, storytelling, and engagement between people.

This is perhaps the trickiest step in your data framework. Depending on how your colleagues and customers view data today, you might need to drive some serious culture change. This is where having a communications lead comes in. They can turn your company and data mission statements into a bigger story about how teams across your business execute that mission using data the right way.

This is a great chance to engage designers in your organization as well. They can bring that story to life via empathy grids, service blueprints, and other design assets that your governance board can use to guide their work.

Your Next Step

Having considered how the seven steps of your framework help you manage data more holistically, use the following template to fulfill these principles within your own organization. This template will guide your next step, which is to assign leadership of each part of this framework to a colleague (or colleagues) in your organization.

You might realize that you don't have enough colleagues in-house for one person to own each aspect of the framework. In that case, denote which parts of the framework can double up due to employee skillsets.

For example, if you're the CTO of a government contracting firm, you might assign the full framework to your Data Practice lead, who can implement the framework across client projects. If your organization is too small to have a full data practice, this might be a good chance to bring in subcontractors who can fill framework gaps on projects as needed, like hiring a firm with cybersecurity expertise to support a client project if you lack enough in-house talent. This list of data leaders will be the basis for your data stewardship plan, which we'll cover in the next chapter.

The toughest part of any big goal is getting started. Having finished this chapter and the work within it, you are off to an awesome start. You confirmed your organization's mission statement and considered how data can achieve it. You wrote a proposed mission statement to use data, and started applying a data governance framework in the context of your own business. This is a lot of hard, necessary work. It speaks volumes about your tenacity and drive to use data well.

The seven-step framework you've just reviewed is only as good as the people who will bring it to life. Your next task is to engage them.

CHAPTER 2

Select Data Stewards

Andrew Ng is a machine learning (ML) pioneer. He co-founded and served as Head of Google Brain, built the Artificial Intelligence group at Baidu, and co-founded Coursera, alongside his work as an adjunct professor at Stanford. When Ng gives advice on the state of ML, people listen. And his assessment of the industry's future shows some gaps to fill.[1]

"When a system isn't performing well, many teams instinctually try to improve the Code," Ng writes. "But for many practical applications, it's more effective instead to focus on improving the Data." Ng elaborates that historically, ML progressed through efforts to improve code while researchers held the data fixed in benchmark datasets. To see significant progress in the future, teams must put their data quality first. Rather than prioritizing code-centric models, Ng says tech leaders must make systemic changes to the data that powers these models.

While this is an admirable goal, it's also challenging. Today's businesses have more data than they know what to do with. On top of that, the average CTO's schedule is full as-is. How can you ensure data quality at all stages of every data pipeline?

The good news is you don't have to do it alone. The businesses with successful data projects build teams of data stewards to help them reach this goal. Choosing and engaging data stewards across all lines of business yields diverse teams that give colleagues agency and autonomy. In this chapter, you'll become familiar with the key role data stewards play in your data governance strategy, and how they'll help you fulfill the framework discussed in Chapter 1, Find Your Data Framework, on page 1.

---

1. https://read.deeplearning.ai/the-batch/issue-84/

Before we go on, I want to address the agile elephant in the room. As someone who works in environments that prize continuous development,[2] I'm aware that finding data stewards for a company-wide council can seem bureaucratic. Worse than that, it can seem fully divorced from your daily execution.

In Chapter 4, Write Your Data Roadmap, on page 43 you'll explore tactics to bake data governance into your roadmap, requirements, and other key tasks you will execute per sprint. Done well, data governance is how your organization delivers data projects faster and of higher quality than your competition. It's also the series of strategic steps your teams take to make each sprint more productive than the last. But you can't make each sprint look flawless without the right data stewards to lead them.

By the end of this chapter, you will be able to identify colleagues in your organization who are experts in various data domains and can help bring your data governance to life. These colleagues will be your data stewards.

What Are Data Stewards?

Data stewards own the strategic and tactical decisions for data within their respective business domains. Stewards serve as trusted advisors for their data, providing key context and nuance as needed. For example, a director of customer success could serve as a data steward by owning and offering key insights about customer data that your business prioritizes, like average response time and the number of new accounts per month.

You might wonder if data stewards must hold technical roles. After all, data scientists, engineers, and similar roles work with all types of data each day. Aren't they most qualified to serve as stewards? The answer is sometimes, but not always.

Data stewards bring their own unique value to your business. This includes deep knowledge of the company strategy, customer pain points, collaboration processes, and cultural nuances. By working in a diverse range of roles, they lead areas of the business that your data team might touch tangentially, if at all. Perhaps most crucially, data stewards are experts in their unique domains, whether that be sales, marketing, product, or legal. This knowledge is invaluable to colleagues in data engineering, data science, and data architecture; they need those insights to support their own work.

For example, let's say your data team must re-design the taxonomy within a database about cars. Before that content reaches its database, a team of

---

2.   https://www.atlassian.com/continuous-delivery/principles/continuous-integration-vs-delivery-vs-deployment

statisticians collects, downloads, cleans, and analyzes the data for their specific products. This expertise varies per statistician. Whereas one statistician owns the data for BMWs, another owns the data for Audis.

Database users tell your user research team that it's too hard for them to find the data they need within this database. To help users get more value from your database, your data team must redesign the taxonomies for BMW and Audi products. Before your data team can start this crucial work, they'll need several questions answered:

- How is the data for these commodities collected?

- Who collects this data, and where is it stored before it reaches the user database?

- How many databases does this data live in? Are they on-premise or cloud databases?

- How often is new commodity data released to the public?

- How are these car-specific data releases prepared, and who prepares them?

- Is this preparation process automated, manual, or both?

- Which quality assurance checks do statisticians use, and which colleagues participate in these processes?

To find accurate answers to these questions, your team will rely on statisticians who can steward their respective data. (In this case, data about Audi and BMW vehicles.) These stewards will work with your data team to help them learn the answers. Data stewards could help your data team do the following tasks:

Define attributes

Data attributes (also known as metadata) define properties of objects, elements, or files. Data stewards are often the best people to write, manage, and share attributes for the data in their domains. For example, a customer service director might manage details such as customer IDs, addresses, and purchase histories. If this director serves as a customer data steward, they can keep clean, organized, secure records of this data to share with colleagues as needed.

Build data models

If data stewards lack a data architect's expertise, they can still help architects with their work. For example, a data architect who's redesigning a database will need to understand the IT systems that this database must integrate with. A steward who manages these systems can give crucial context to help the architect build better architecture that supports the right integrations, taxonomies, and so on.

Create data dictionaries

Think of data dictionaries as centralized spots for information about data. A great data dictionary helps a system's users find all the details about data that they need in one place. Data stewards can play a key role contributing to these dictionaries as writers, editors, and advisors.

Not all data stewards serve the same function. Where possible, it helps to categorize data stewards as serving either business or technical roles. Separating data stewards into business vs. technical stewards might sound intuitive, but it's often a big roadblock on organizations' data governance journeys.

No matter how nimble a business thinks it is, the truth is that all but the smallest teams have more silos than they think. This leaves most teams with little to no knowledge of how their colleagues in other departments work, or what they work on. And nothing reveals those gaps quite like searching for the right subject matter experts to fill decision-making roles about data.

This is also a hard task because many data stewards lack the autonomy to make organizational change. Despite their status as experts of the data in their domains, they often lack the power to make choices that affect the business strategy. At best, they've built strong relationships with those who have organizational sway, and they can effectively persuade these colleagues to consider their advice. At worst, their advice languishes. To avoid this, a big part of your job will involve giving your stewards the visibility and recognition they deserve.

You'll get some tips on how to do that soon. For now, here's a quick overview of how business data stewardship roles differ from technical roles:

Business stewards own data for business processes and workflows. They own the data classification scheme for data and metadata which falls under their areas of expertise. For example, in our car database, a statistician who produces data releases for BMWs would serve as a steward for BMWs' taxonomic hierarchies. This involves these tasks:

- Collaborating with colleagues to make sure that these hierarchies are accurate, organized, informative, and intuitive

- Collecting data and confirming that this data/metadata meets organizational quality standards

- Reviewing and assessing current taxonomies for commodity line items
- Writing the documentation required for these commodity line items
- Leading data governance trainings for their departments
- Defining, developing, and conducting data quality assessments against pre-defined business metrics

Technical stewards own data for systems, pipelines, and implementation. These stewards help colleagues learn how to model, create, maintain, and transfer data between systems. Technical data stewardship tasks might be these:

- Maintain all requirements for system implementations.
- Manage data marts, data warehouses, data lakes, and data mesh.
- Build and integrate the systems mentioned previously.
- Define parameters for metadata.
- Confirm which data they need to assign different types of content or assets.
- Set limits for which data users and admins can work with.
- Move data from an on-premise to a cloud-based environment, or from one cloud environment to another.
- Build data models and algorithms that achieve business priorities.

Within these broad business and technical categories, data stewardship roles get even more specific. As you read the role descriptions that follow, consider them all within the context of the data framework you referenced in Chapter 1, Find Your Data Framework, on page 1. Your data stewardship team will fulfill this framework by owning data in specific business and technical domains.

All lines of business which produce and/or manage unique data should have designated data stewards. Sales, marketing, and customer success are three teams which manage data that keeps your business running. You should thus have at least one senior member of each team serving as a data steward who can own the data in their respective business domains.

Your business might need more or fewer stewards than this list, which is fine; adapt your stewards to your own business needs and restrictions. The key takeaway is that any stewardship role should align with at least one aspect of the seven-part data framework. With that in mind, here's a non-exhaustive list of roles that data stewards can serve:

Council Chair Data Steward

Your data stewardship council chair plays its key leadership role. The chair leads all meetings with stewards and represents the data governance council at meetings with folks throughout the business. The council chair approves requests to start projects or buy new data tools, leads meetings with the data governance council about its direction, and owns the data governance strategy. At a high level, they perform the following tasks:

- Build and implement a strategic data management plan for data governance council members to execute.

- Oversee all projects and initiatives related to organizational data.

- Assign responsibilities to data stewards for respective technical and business roles.

- Share communication about changes to data initiatives.

- Represent the data governance council at C-suite and cross-departmental meetings.

- Explain the organization's response to security breaches.

- Define what "quality data" means in your organization, including which data sources to use and avoid.

Security Data Steward

Security data stewards set data usage and security policies in partnership with the data governance council chair and C-suite. Security data stewards liaise between the business and technical sides of your organization to set and share security updates throughout the broader business.

Security stewards perform the following tasks:

- Oversee all security requirements to safeguard data.

- Assign appropriate security classifications to all company data based on sensitivity.

- Collect all security-related data artifacts for legacy and new projects.

- Create security artifacts as needed.

- Assess current security requirements, and adherence to these requirements.

- Make security findings available on request.

- Define data lockup requirements.

- Conduct gap and impact analyses of all new security requirements.

- Compare security requirements against current and proposed data environments.

- Audit and approve all proposed production changes against security risks.

Your security data steward should review any new project or tool that your council approves. They'll assess each request against the organization's security standards, offering guidance early to avoid technical debt.

Ethics and Transparency Data Steward

This steward ensures your data governance policies meet the clear, defensible, and documented standards discussed for data use in Transparency and Ethics, on page 8. Your ethics and transparency data steward works directly with the data team to help data analysts, scientists, architects, and engineers consider how their work might impact customers in unintended ways.

The ethics and transparency data steward might do hands-on work with data if they have a data science or engineering background, but this isn't required to drive change in the role. Your ethics and transparency data steward will need to consider a broad range of digital ethics risks per data project, then share those risks with the data governance council. An ethics and transparency data steward should perform these tasks:

- Write compliance standards for how your organization stores, shares, collects, and protects data.

- Map possible ethics risks per data project back to your organization's business and data mission statements.

- Document decisions for how to manage data, including rationale for how these decisions serve the business and customers alike. (This is especially important, as customer well-being often stands at odds with what's "best" for the business.)

- Train employees across the organization to practice data ethics, from C-suite leaders to individual contributors.

- Ensure that your organization's data ethics practice meets broader legal and legislative compliance standards.

- Confirm that all technology your business buys and uses meets your organization's own compliance standards.

Many ethics and transparency stewards have backgrounds in law and/or compliance, which helps them assess risk and predict which data use might breach civil rights.

Documentation Data Steward

Your documentation data steward is your council's resident writer. They manage the council's documentation repository, which stores everything from council meeting notes to business requirements for user acceptance testing per project. Within this stewardship role, they perform these tasks:

- Write consistent data definitions.

- Train colleagues across the organization on best practices to document data-based work.

- Store this documentation in the appropriate area(s).

- Write, edit, and manage documentation for all data-based decisions and initiatives.

- Manage artifacts like data architecture diagrams, data model(s), and data dictionaries.

- Edit data artifacts as needed in partnership with technical stewards.

- Organize all high-level data assets, such as data dictionaries and metadata catalogs.

This data steward might not write all the documentation themselves; part of a data governance council's value is having folks across the business own data-specific work so it doesn't fall to one person. In cases where they don't write documentation themselves, the documentation data steward still owns the repository and stores documentation appropriately.

Compliance Data Steward

Compliance data stewards often bring legal backgrounds to their data governance work. This steward tracks regulatory changes involving data and ensures data usage meets those changes. They work closely with all roles on the data stewardship council, from writing compliance standards for the documentation data steward to reviewing data transparency requirements with your ethics data steward. The compliance data steward performs these tasks:

- Reviews regulatory frameworks for data across markets where your business serves users.

- Interprets diverse laws to confirm data-specific rights for businesses and consumers.

- Ensures that your business follows essential laws for data management per project and vendor selection.

- Communicates with data stewards and the data team to ensure that everyone considers compliance pre-resource allocation.

- Reviews models during the data use life cycle to ensure that the data team follows data quality standards before, during, and after production.

If some of these titles sound familiar, it's because key stewardship roles align with the data governance framework you explored in Find Your Data Governance Framework, on page 5. When building your own data stewardship team, make sure you have alignment between stewardship roles and the respective parts of your data framework. Assigning colleagues to co-own your framework will help bring it to life.

Depending on your organization's size, you might not have enough stewards to fill roles that address all aspects of the framework. In those cases, look for opportunities where one steward has the expertise to own two parts of the framework. For instance, there's a lot of natural overlap between the ethics and transparency data steward and the compliance data steward. If you have an attorney on staff to serve as the compliance steward, ethics and transparency can fall to them as well.

When trying to fill roles per part of the framework, consider who's already doing this work. A data steward who leads customer success could be the ideal fit for your education and training data steward role. This empowers them to help all colleagues in your organization learn what data governance is, why it's relevant to everyone's roles, and how to ask data stewards for help. Customer success teams spend their days speaking to clients, triaging questions, and showing diverse people how to use your products. Education and training is already a key aspect of their work. This aptitude puts them in a natural spot to steward education and training for data governance.

Likewise, a marketing leader can serve as your collaboration and culture data steward. Marketers explore, create, and lead opportunities to find the right audience for your products. The best marketers are natural storytellers who can seamlessly share how their products meet your needs. You will need that storytelling prowess to share why data governance is a team sport, and guide your company culture through the change required to make it work long-term.

You will know your data stewardship council is on the right track when each aspect of the seven-part framework is accounted for. But if you're still in the early stages, you might wonder how to hire data stewards at all. The great news is that you don't have to.

Fill Your Council with the Right People

Data stewards don't need to be hired from elsewhere; that is one of their biggest benefits. Unlike data scientists, who are often expensively recruited, data stewards are already part of your business. As a result, they bring deep knowledge of your tech stack, strategy, and customer pain points to their daily work. Data stewards aren't just nice to have, nor should they replace trained data scientists. They bring their own unique value to your business and are equally essential.

This bears repeating since it's no longer enough for one employee to own all data-based decisions—or for your business to avoid investing in the tools, training, and employees who can take your data usage to the next level. Achieving this demands a larger, more cross-functional team that makes shared decisions about data and collaborates across silos.

So, you don't need to hire data stewards, but you do need to find them. The amount of time and resources this takes will vary depending on your organization's size, and the scope of each person's role.

For example, it's not uncommon for a startup employee to lead both marketing and product in the early years. Depending on the size of this marketing/product leader's staff, one person might own data in both the marketing and product departments. As a result, you might easily find a strong steward, only to realize that person has limited time to help.

If you work for a large organization, it's more likely that your staff of knowledge experts works in silos away from each other. In these situations, it's common for one person to hold specific knowledge about their domain. If this domain is a subject like security, it can be an easy expertise match for your stewardship team. But finding that match can take time via endless emails, introductions, and calendar invites. You might think you've found the data steward you need, only to meet them and realize you'll need to speak with someone else instead.

So, you'll want to be strategic about how to find the right data stewards. Before you start searching internally for them, answer the following questions:

How Big Is My Organization's Product Suite?

Consider your data needs within the larger context of your organization. How many products and services does your business offer? Does each product or service have its own customer base? The answers to these questions will give you a sense of how large your data stewardship council should be.

Let's go back to the car database example. If your data team is tasked with redesigning a database taxonomy, that might seem like you're working to improve a single project with fixed deadlines and staff/data stewards who will work on it short-term. But to make lasting, meaningful changes to that database, you'll need to answer these questions first:

- Which systems does this database integrate with and pull data from?
- What's the hierarchy of data like within this database?
- Are there multiple taxonomies within this database?
- Is this database redesign part of a larger digital transformation effort?

If the answer to that final question is "Yes," your data stewardship needs just increased drastically. That is not a bad thing; it gives you a realistic view of the challenge you're tasked with solving *and* a stronger sense of how many data stewards you'll need.

Which Data Do I Need the Most Help With?

Consider the data that's top-of-mind for you while reading this book. Would you classify it as more technical, or on the business side of your organization, or both? Once you've assessed the type(s) of data you're working with, you can look across departments to find the best steward(s) who can own this data.

Your efforts to find stewards will be most successful if you've already built strong relationships with them. Ideally, these stewards are colleagues with whom you've collaborated and built a strong rapport. They know how their work contributes to the bigger business, and want to help your data steward-ship efforts since this work aligns with their own.

There is no singular answer for how many data stewards your business might need. Your own answer will depend on how large your company's product suite is, how long your planned engagement(s) will be, and whether your data project at hand stands on its own or is part of a bigger digital transformation effort. When in doubt, start small. You can always request a steward's help for six months and re-evaluate your needs as the work continues. Since agile projects work in increments, it's natural to bring stewards into your fold as needed.

When asking how many stewards you'll need, it helps to start by writing all your unanswered questions down:

- What are the biggest security risks?
- Which blockers do you foresee on the path to production?
- Whose buy-in from the business do you need?

Once you've written those questions down, categorize them by organizational area, from business and tech to security and project management. The number of areas you identify will give you a strong sense of how many data stewards you'll need, at least in the beginning. When in doubt, recall that the data framework we're using has seven parts. So, aim for seven stewards to get your data governance council off the ground, and assign ownership of the seven framework steps to one steward each.

While stewards can serve dual roles on the data governance council, it's not ideal to spread stewards too thin. You can double up stewardship areas as needed, but avoid assigning them three-plus domains. That gets overwhelming and increases the risk that data quality might suffer.

Write down which insights and expertise you need from each of these seven stewards. Be as specific as possible. Which parts of your data governance framework will each steward own? How does this work complement their daily tasks? Are they responsible for managing specific data in your organization? If so, which data do they manage, where do they store this data, and which data pipelines might you need it for?

Remember that you're selecting stewards for their expertise, and your goal is to leverage that knowledge without creating more work for them. To achieve this, reference the data framework and data mission statement from Chapter 1, Find Your Data Framework, on page 1. When selecting stewards to manage ethics, security, documentation, and so on, look across your business to see who fulfills these roles.

As mentioned earlier in this chapter, your business attorney might be a strong candidate to serve as a data steward for ethics and/or compliance. Likewise, your technical writer is a strong candidate to serve as a documentation data steward.

Regardless of their business or technical skills, the most essential acumen each steward should have is the will to effectively drive change within your culture. You and your stewardship team are about to lead substantial organizational efforts. The next chapter will share how to build and sustain a data governance council with the expertise to transform your business. In the meantime, you might have a more pressing question.

Your Next Step

You know the pros when it comes to collaborating with data stewards. Believe it or not, that's the easy part. Once you've found the right colleagues to serve as stewards, you'll be faced with a more crucial question: "How can I motivate them to help?"

As an organizational leader, finding data stewards has clear benefits for you. It helps you build a multifaceted, cross-functional team that shares responsibilities for data ownership. Your data team gains allies across diverse areas, from marketing to engineering. And you'll get even more resources to help your data efforts.

But all of that's for naught if you can't answer the key question in your stewards' minds: "What's in this for me?"

Data stewards bring great value to your organization. What's less clear at first is how data stewardship benefits stewards themselves. You could be asking your head of sales, senior statistician, or clinical intern to do even more work without any obvious benefits for them.

Your data stewardship program's biggest risk is overloading stewards with even more work, thus breeding resentment and unwillingness to help. To keep stewards engaged for the long haul, you'll need to respect their time and reward their contributions. That involves giving them credit for the work they're putting towards this initiative.

So, your homework for this chapter is to review your stewardship list and make a plan to reward their efforts. These rewards should be tangible, whether through bonuses, increased/discounted stock options, or formally adding stewardship tasks to their job descriptions. This last option positions stewards to exceed expectations in their current roles, making them more likely to get promoted. It rewards expertise they already have and positions them to advance their careers based on sharing their valuable knowledge.

As always, be realistic about what you can do with the resources you have. If your team has an annual budget that doesn't reset until each autumn, plan ahead to reallocate some budget for data steward bonuses. Perhaps you're hiring a new technical writer; if so, work with this person's manager on adding data stewardship duties to their job description. This allows data governance to be a core part of their role, not an add-on.

Both examples assume you're in a position at work to oversee a budget and/or influence big business functions, like hiring. If not, this is your chance to manage up. Whether you're a change management consultant or an in-house data scientist, you are in a position to influence authority. Your client or organization hired you to help them build a better tomorrow because they can't do it on their own.

This does not mean you won't encounter resistance. That's par for the course with the deep work that you're doing. But if you're worried that advocating for data stewards and rewarding them fairly is overstepping, remind yourself that this is what leaders do; they build the best teams they can, then reward them for the hard work they contribute.

In her ode to AI projects that fail, Cassie Kozyrkov, Head of Decision Intelligence at Google, shares[3] that searching for a unicorn is a key reason why most machine learning models don't see the light of day. Kozyrkov says that even if you did find said unicorn who can juggle architecture, engineering, UX, and QA, there's far too much work for them to do it all alone. She offers this alternative:

"Instead of trying to do it all yourself, learn how to check whether the baton was passed between your teammates correctly."

If your organization is truly data-driven, it's not enough to hire a handful of experts and let them work away from the rest of the business. Being data-driven means prioritizing data quality and engaging everyone to co-own it. If each company today is a data company, then every employee is a data steward. And if every employee's a data steward, you'll need their buy-in to pass the baton.

You've made great strides towards achieving this goal. The work you've done selecting data stewards in your business puts you in strong shape to build your data governance council. With the right stewardship team in place, you're poised to build a council that can use data to drive lasting change. Chapter 3 will show you how.

---

3.   https://towardsdatascience.com/3-signs-that-your-ai-project-is-doomed-9e3ab82d9425

CHAPTER 3

Build Your Data Governance Council

In October 2021, the United States Department of Agriculture (USDA) released a plan to tackle climate change. Clocking in at 40 pages, the agency's climate adaptation and resilience plan explains how the agency will help agricultural producers build resilience for an increasingly erratic climate.

In its press release announcing this plan, USDA said, "The plan is part of USDA's response to Executive Order 14008, Tackling the Climate Crisis at Home and Abroad, which tasked all federal agencies with preparing action plans for integrating climate adaptation into their missions, programs, operations, and management."

As I learned how this new plan will affect the agency, I was struck by the Executive Order's decree for all agencies to integrate climate adaptation into their DNA. Since I was in the thick of data governance research, I couldn't help but notice how this new plan might serve as a model for great data governance.

First, this plan addressed the President's Executive Order on Tackling the Climate Crisis at Home and Abroad. The U.S. President declared climate change to be a widespread problem that the government should tackle from the top down across all USDA agencies. To ensure that this goal remained top-of-mind, leadership tasked all agencies with making climate adaptation a key part of their work.

While climate change itself might not have much to do with data, USDA's governance model does. Their approach emphasizes how crucial it is to have top-down support for an initiative that scales across teams. It's worth highlighting since this way of working is still not the norm.

Typically, when companies start new initiatives, they put all the work for that initiative on one team or department. They hire a new chief, task them with transforming the whole business while wielding minimal power, often give that chief an underwhelming budget, and keep their initiatives confined to that team. Approaching digital transformations this way ensures that their work will have minimal impact.

This chapter will show you how to do the opposite. You will learn how to form a cross-functional data stewardship council that drives real change in your organization. At the end of this chapter, you'll know why the right sponsor makes or breaks your council, when your newly formed council should meet, and which data efforts to prioritize first. You will have a way to resolve roadblocks, measure success, and govern data on the way to production.

Remember, the biggest barriers to building data governance aren't technical, they're cultural. Ninety-two percent of mainstream companies in one survey said that when it comes to launching data projects in their organizations, they still struggle with challenges that range from learning new business processes to resistance against change.[1] You are designing your organization's first data governance plan, which means you're introducing a lot of change. Here's how to create a council that will champion this change.

Find the Most Effective Sponsor

We've all dealt with meeting fatigue where colleagues try to solve problems by filling our calendar with invitations to "hop on a quick call." If meetings lack purpose, agendas, clear leaders, or follow-up actions, they could've been emails and saved endless hours. One less-discussed time suck? Not having the right people in the room to make key decisions.

You've done lots of work thus far to select the right data stewards for your data governance council. All of it will stall if you don't have a senior member of your organization to sponsor this council and its data governance efforts. So, your first step is to confirm whom you'll need sponsorship from.

Imagine you're in a C-suite role yourself as the Chief Data Officer (CDO). You might report to the Chief Information Officer (CIO) or the Chief Executive Officer (CEO). Your role involves writing the strategy to collect, store, and manage your organization's data. All of this work is data governance, and since you're part of the executive team, you might be the perfect person to lead the data governance council by serving the board chair stewardship role that we'll discuss below.

If you're in a C-suite role yourself, do you need more executive buy-in? The answer depends on your unique business, the company culture, and your

---

1.   https://hbr.org/2021/02/why-is-it-so-hard-to-become-a-data-driven-company

own relationship with the rest of the executives. If you report to the CIO, your boss owns the infrastructure for your organization. Their tasks include signing off on procurement for new tech, implementing new IT across the organization, and ensuring that all IT decisions support the business strategy.

Now, consider the work your data governance council will do. You'll start by selecting a specific, data-focused project to shepherd through production. To achieve this goal, your data stewards will need to choose the right tech stack, build processes to confirm data quality, ensure that all data meets security standards, and document a strategy to prevent data drift post-production, amongst other tasks.

Since this work falls under the CIO's domain, your data governance council will need the CIO's buy-in. But you've glimpsed your boss's calendar and know how slammed they are. Adding council chairperson duties to their list won't likely go well. In this case, asking them to serve as your council's sponsor is a great option.

Sponsors are discussed less often than mentors, but their role is more essential. Sponsors advocate for your work by ensuring that it gets the resources and visibility to thrive. This saves huge amounts of time in the long run. Rather than spending months searching for buy-in only to realize you've recruited the wrong people, you'll confirm that your data governance council's work has support from someone with the power and connections to advocate for that work, even when your councilmembers are not in the room.

Whoever your council sponsor is, you will need to sell them on your data governance efforts. Remember the data mission statement that you wrote in Chapter 1? It's going to come in handy here. Since you'll be appealing to business leaders, you'll need to show that your data governance efforts support their goals. All the work you did in Chapter 1, from writing your mission statement for data to assigning stewards per section of your framework, should reinforce a bigger business goal. Whatever that goal is, from decreasing overhead to boosting customer satisfaction, you'll find the right sponsor for your data governance council if you show that your work will improve theirs.

If you're not sure how to choose the right sponsor for your council, it helps to follow this guidance from Sylvia Ann Hewlett: "Would-be sponsors in large organizations are ideally two levels above you with line of sight to your role; in smaller firms, they're either the founder or president or are part of his or her inner circle."[2]

---

2.   https://hbr.org/2013/09/the-right-way-to-find-a-career-sponsor

As you read this advice, consider your own organizational structure. Whether you're in the C-suite or below, finding the right sponsor for your council will require you to manage up. The best way to do that is to find senior leaders in your organization who grasp how crucial data is for your business, are familiar with your work, and have strong relationships with colleagues across the business. Most crucially, they're committed to giving your council the buy-in, resources, and sponsorship to succeed. Their help is essential to not letting your work languish.

Convince Colleagues to Join Your Council

Remote work's rise during the Covid-19 pandemic further blurred the thin line between work and home. Six months into the pandemic, Harvard Business School research found that the average workday was now 48.5 minutes longer.[3] The average employee surveyed in this study joined 13 percent more meetings than they did pre-pandemic. I know that these constant check-ins, scrum standups, and Slack pings distract me like nothing else. I'm doing my best to join fewer meetings, not more.

This matters because employees are exhausted, including your colleagues. Between work and family obligations, their calendars are likely overbooked already. When colleagues already struggle to do heads-down work during business hours, you'll need to show them what they'll gain by joining the council. Luckily, this doesn't have to be as hard as you might think.

To start, don't underestimate the fear of missing out (FOMO). It's why we attend all these meetings to start with.[4] In an increasingly globalized workforce, Western work culture still equates presence with productivity. People worry that if they decline meetings invites, they will lose their abilities to influence the business.

This is not an excuse to triple book your colleagues with data governance meetings. That said, the psychological importance placed on meetings means that folks want their voices heard, especially when it affects their own work.

That raises my second point: data is a team sport that all colleagues must join. I recall completing my journalism internships in high school and college, giddy at the thought of not needing to measure my work's worth in numbers. Less than a decade later, my digital articles lived and died by Google Analytics. No matter your role, data plays a part, even if your work is more qualitative.

---

3. https://hbswk.hbs.edu/item/you-re-right-you-are-working-longer-and-attending-more-meetings
4. https://hbr.org/2021/11/the-psychology-behind-meeting-overload

But to quote Maximilian Faschan, formerly of the Oxford Internet Institute, not everyone has equal say over data's impact on their work:[5]

> "In the current reality, data exploration is in the hands of a small group of specialists crunching data on everybody else's behalf while most employees have to watch from the side-line until their analytical demands are being served. In this largely transactional setup, the confidence with which employees rely on data, the speed with which analytical requests are executed and the number of analytical requests that can be served at any given point in time are strictly dependent on the number of specialists available."

The traditional hierarchy involves data flowing down from the CIO's office, with the IT security team controlling all departments' access to it. This approach often fails because folks are less open to rules thrust upon them, especially if they had no say in creating them and can't see how these rules improve their own work. So, when you approach prospective data stewards to join your council, emphasize the power that joining offers them. Each data steward serving on the council should have these things:

- Recognition that they're experts of their functional domains. If colleagues have questions about specific types of data, they should know whom to ask and acknowledge each steward's unique expertise.

- Input regarding decisions about data that affect the organization. Each steward should also have clearly defined freedom to work with the council's chair on matters that impact their own data domains.

- Autonomy to build data quality standards within their data domains

- Freedom to collaborate cross-functionally with colleagues who own different data domains

- Rewards for assuming a leadership role advancing data governance in the organization

If you manage a budget, consider allotting some of it to bonuses per steward. Likewise, find alignment between each steward's role and their work on the council. If their data governance contributions go beyond each steward's scope of work, you can offer to write mid-year and/or year-end reviews per steward. This formally recognizes the work each steward does and positions them to advance in their careers. For instance, if a steward who holds a business role wants to pursue a data-based role full time, your review of their stewardship work can speed up their transition.

---

5.   https://towardsdatascience.com/what-if-data-became-everybodys-business-85b7c20d6ab7

The common threads are leadership, visibility, and the autonomy to do impactful work. The point is not to make these data governance council meetings the only place where stewards are seen and heard. Rather, your goal as council chair is to give each data steward the resources they need to own data each day, throughout their data domains' life cycles.

Clarify the Cadence for Your Council Meetings

I once pitched a data governance council as part of my team's data strategy proposal. During the first meeting with our client, we shared why a council of cross-functional data stewards is the best way to manage data standards and lead agency-wide adoption of those standards. Upon sharing our pitch, my team was thrilled to hear our client say that they agreed with our approach. Still, they had a few questions about the execution: how much time would stewards spend on this work, and how could we ensure that they'd make meaningful contributions while taking care not to burn out?

I think this question should be top-of-mind as you build your own data governance council. My client asked these questions because they needed to sell data governance—and a council to lead it—across their agency. Although my client held a C-suite data role, they didn't manage the business writ large. They needed to lead without direct authority. And, knowing their colleagues as they did, my client had to share the time commitment that stewards could expect.

I bet you've faced this challenge as well. Maybe you're a CIO who must persuade all colleagues to use company technology in appropriate ways. Perhaps you're a junior consultant who must persuade your client why tech adoption sans strategy won't work in the long run. No matter your role, you will need to lead without authority at some point. To do this well, you must design solutions that answer your colleague's key problems.

When convincing data stewards to join your data governance council, lack of time is likely a big blocker. If colleagues decline to serve stewardship roles, it's often because they don't believe it's worth their time or they think they don't have time. You must account for this in your pitch to prospective stewards. You'll succeed if you are honest about the time commitment and share how joining the council will improve their current roles.

When building your council from the ground up, it's ideal to meet at least every other week. The lion's share of policy, process, and procedural work occurs in this early stage, and you'll need commitment from all stewards involved. This work sets the stage for all data governance efforts from now on.

Let's say your data team wants to migrate datasets from an on-premise environment into a cloud-based environment next year. They will need a set of standards they can follow to uphold data quality, privacy, and integrity. For instance, if your data engineers find a dataset that has metadata with personally identifiable information, they'll need to know how they should handle that problem. While they can complete this migration without such standards (most teams do), this increases the risk that your data will be subpar.

All stewards serving on your data governance council must view this work as an investment in the business and their roles within it. Once your council lays the first foundation, it pays dividends by giving all colleagues a clear set of standards to use for their benefit. Until then, ensure that your council gives this work the time it deserves. That should involve meeting for at least 60 minutes every other week. Between meetings, stewards should expect to contribute one to four hours of work towards achieving the key tasks covered throughout this chapter.

When sharing this news, recall that you've selected data stewards because their roles align with the work required to make key decisions about data in their domains. While serving on the council requires commitment, this work should align with stewards' current tasks and goals. If your senior marketing director will serve as a steward leading the collaboration and culture aspect of your data framework, this fits into their work attracting the right user base for your organization's products. Each steward's job exists to grow and improve your organization. Since strong data governance achieves that goal, each steward's manager should adjust stewards' workloads to prioritize this.

See why council sponsors are so crucial? To give this council the time and resources it needs to thrive, you'll need governance to be a top-down effort. Data stewards and their bosses won't support the data governance council without knowing it's approved and prioritized by senior leadership. If you prioritize sponsorship buy-in, ensure that each steward is the right fit to lead aspects of the data framework, and share how stewards' council work enhances their own, you can design a response that addresses the time crunch.

Confirm Key Principles for Your Council

If you gain one message from this book, I hope it's that all your data governance work should have higher purpose. The hype around data, coupled with how quickly it's created, leads most organizations to greenlight data projects without the right strategy for them to succeed. A 2021 executive survey[6] by NewVantage Partners found that while 92 percent of surveyed firms reported investing in big data and AI initiatives faster, most companies either failed to make progress or even lost progress managing data as a business asset. A mere 29 percent achieved transformational business outcomes with data, while fewer than one in four said their company was data-driven within the past year—a decline from 37.8 percent the year before.

With your data governance council in place, you're prepared to beat these odds. The next step is to write down what your council will do. These principles define the scope of work for your council and its stewards. They help everyone know why this council exists and what it will work on. These principles also help colleagues who don't serve on the council have key points of contact for specific data questions.

If you're stuck on which principles to start with, consider how other organizations manage data. Universities often have published, well-defined data governance principles, given how much data they own. Some, like Washington University in St. Louis, have whole websites devoted to data governance that anyone can read. Wash U. does a strong job defining who sits on its data governance council and what they're responsible for:[7]

> "The Data Governance Council is comprised of Data Administrators and other senior officials who have planning, policy-level and management responsibility for data within their functional areas. The Data Governance Office will be ex-officio members.
>
> The Data Governance Council will:
>
> - Review and approve data governance policy, standards, guidelines, and procedures
> - Further the overall vision and guiding principles of data governance
> - Resolve issues escalated by Data Stewards
> - Escalate issues to the Executive IT Committee
> - Monitor and review overall Data Governance Program
> - Hold ongoing meetings"

Washington University's data governance website shows they have an Executive IT Governance Committee as well. If your own organization has a similar committee, this is the ideal place to search for sponsorship. This executive committee can push your data governance efforts forward by serving in stewardship roles or by helping you find stewards as the needs arise. They can also remove blockers to getting council work done, and greenlight new projects.

---

6.   https://c6abb8db-514c-4f5b-b5a1-fc710f1e464e.filesusr.com/ugd/ e5361a_76709448ddc6490981f0cbea42d51508.pdf

7.   https://data.wustl.edu/data-governance/stewardship/

Work with what you've got in-house; one organization's council principles might not match your own. The point is to write principles that clearly define what your data governance council does and why it exists.

Incorporating your data mission statement into your principles is a strong starting point. Likewise, when writing your council's principles, consider having each principle reflect one part of your data governance framework. If you follow this model, you'll write seven principles based on the framework from Chapter 1:

- Trust
- Transparency and Ethics
- Values and Outcomes
- Risk and Security
- Accountability and Decision Rights
- Collaboration and Culture
- Education and Training

A set of data governance principles written in service of that framework might be as follows:

- "Use and uphold data in a clear, consistent manner that inspires trust amongst our colleagues and customers."

- "Be transparent about our data use and keep ethics at the forefront of our data standards."

- "Consider end outcomes (both good and bad) of data use to ensure that data upholds our values."

- "Plan ahead for risk and secure our data at all stages of each pipeline."

- "Take accountability for why, when, how, and who makes decisions about data."

- "Collaborate to build a company-wide culture that prioritizes data."

- "Educate our colleagues about big data and train everyone to stewards data in their domains."

Anyone in your organization who uses business data needs principles to inform how they'll use it and who owns it. To help them, publish your data governance principles in a shared space where all colleagues can access them. Since part of your framework involves risk and security, you'll work with your data stewards to define the level of security per data domain. But when it comes to sharing your data governance framework and principles, no one should doubt what those are or have trouble accessing them.

The more transparent your principles are, the more trustworthy your data governance council will become. Since you aim to inspire trust amongst customers and colleagues alike, I suggest following Wash U.'s lead and publishing your data governance principles on your organization's website. When everyone knows which values your organization uses to keep data clean, safe, and accurate, they can make a more well-informed choice about whether to do business with you.

Define Data Domains

Now that you've reviewed your data's mission statement, recall the list of data stewards you created in Chapter 2, Select Data Stewards, on page 13. You've identified which colleagues are best suited to serve each potential stewardship role so you can all bring this mission statement to life. These stewards should understand the company culture, goals, and how their work upholds it. Once they've agreed to serve on the data governance council, your next step is to work with each steward on defining the data domain(s) they will own.

Data domains are logical groups of data that address a common purpose, concept, or object. It helps to think of every department in your organization as its own data domain, each with its own subdomains. For example, human resources (HR) is one data domain.[8] Within that domain, HR data has several subdomains like Recruiting, Onboarding, Time Tracking, and Benefits.[9] The exact number of data domains depends on your industry. The article "What is a data domain" by George Firican offers the following examples:

In the education sector, you might have:

- Student
- Research
- Faculty
- Alumni
- Advancement

In the healthcare sector, you might have:

- Patient
- Facility
- Medical procedure

---

8. https://www.lightsondata.com/what-is-a-data-domain-examples-included/
9. https://data.wustl.edu/data-governance/data-domains/

In the insurance sector, you might encounter:

- Provider
- Member

Any of these sectors could have some of the previous data domains as well. So for example, I'm sure that all 3 sectors would all have 'Location', 'Transaction', and 'Legal' as data domains.

Data domains define the model schema and other attributes for each respective business area. You might choose to have data domains for customers, employees, and products. The stewards who oversee each domain will define the attributes, format, and metadata which confirms how domains should expect to store the data. This last part is crucial since your data governance council must standardize how it will exchange data between systems.

Within databases, a data element is the collection of values that data elements may contain. Your databases must know how to store and categorize data across the business. So, your data governance council must make binary standards that data can fit into.

Let's revisit the healthcare data domains. If you think of these data domains as a drop-down menu, you will see this list:

- Patient
- Facility
- Medical procedure
- Location
- Transaction
- Legal

Within a database, all data should align with one of these six data domains, and any new data should map up to one of the six. A key part of data governance involves correctly categorizing data within all organizational systems, and keeping it consistent across systems. So, each data steward will need to build their data domains by choosing how to categorize it. This includes categorizing data according to domains and relevant sub-domains.

Sub-domains help data stewards categorize data at a more granular level. If you've chosen Patient as a data domain, you can create sub-domains according to the types of patients (infants, children, geriatric, and so on). The steward per data domain will need to define each relevant sub-domain, ensuring a relationship between each sub-domain and its parent.

It helps to think of sub-domains as types of data domains. If you've chosen Facility as a data domain, consider the types of facilities your business engages. That will help you choose appropriate sub-domains which you can use to categorize facility data.

Specifics per domain and sub-domain vary across industries and organizations. Whatever you and your data stewards choose, recall that your goal is to create consistent grouping conventions for essential data types that apply across enterprise-wide business units (culture) and systems (technical).

Throughout my career in tech, I've encountered roadblocks where teams within the same organization define the same data differently. I've also seen naming conventions that differ based on which department I'm engaging, even if we are all discussing the same data. Having your data governance council define data domains and sub-domains is hugely important to avoid this blocker. It establishes your data governance council and stewards as a single source of truth for this information.

Per Wash U., these are some principles to follow when defining data domains:

- Each [domain] is aligned with a business function, like Research, Clinical, etc.
- Not a system or an application (Workday, Epic, RMS)
- Each domain has one administrator
- Each domain will determine who has access to data within that domain

Once you and your stewards define data domains and sub-domains, you will need to write it all down. That's where a data dictionary will come in.

Write a Data Dictionary

A data dictionary stores information about data that lives in all your organization's systems. It gives everyone a shared vocabulary for how to discuss data in your organization. Whether it's the CEO, a developer, or a customer service representative, everyone should reference the data dictionary when they're unsure what certain data items mean. This dictionary is a comprehensive space to define rules, regulations, and definitions for your organization's data.

Data dictionaries play a key role in your governance efforts. They reinforce data domains/sub-domains and help teams avoid inconsistencies with data. Having more consistent data makes it easier to analyze, because it gives everyone shared understanding of what different terms mean. Data dictionaries also help your data governance council share data standards—rules that explain how to collect, record, and socialize data—with everyone in your organization.

You might wonder how a data dictionary differs from a business glossary. Glossaries have key terms with names and definitions. Subject matter experts write glossaries with business users in mind, so readers shouldn't need high levels of technical acumen. Business glossaries can document metadata associated with terms in the dictionary. That said, data dictionaries have some key distinctions from these glossaries.

Data dictionaries document relationships[10] between data elements, like data's origins, descriptions, and how they're used relative to each other. The details in data dictionaries allow members of technical teams, like developers and data scientists, to share knowledge with each other and communicate quickly. These details include data structure, type, format, and length.

As your data governance council's chair, you'll track when folks submit new terms and ensure that your whole organization can access these changes to the data dictionary. Each data steward will manage terms for their respective data domains by soliciting terms, ensuring they're correct, submitting them to the data dictionary, and editing as needed. As council chair, you'll define relationships between elements; stewards define what those elements are.

If you're not sure where to start, look at a database your organization uses. Data dictionaries act like catalogs that show how data inside databases relates to each other. These dictionaries grow in importance as you build your analytics stack. Once you start integrating data systems and warehouses, you'll need to know which data lives in each environment, and how it relates to other data.

I've worked on projects with data dictionaries that were incomplete or nonexistent. Since my team's job was to build our client a new data model, the client's lack of knowledge about which data lived where, when new data deployed to different environments, and what certain terms meant caused a nightmare. Our team figured it out once they gained system access, but if they had this information sooner, we could have moved to production even faster.

To avoid this, check if your database has a data dictionary. Many systems have space for data dictionaries built in. If so, use that space to document your own work rather than storing your data dictionary in a separate tool. Your data governance council's work will flow most smoothly if you keep your work stored in as few places as possible.

Data projects have a lot of moving parts, and your data stewards have a lot on their plates. So, review each database your business uses to store data and confirm if they have data dictionaries. If so, use these spaces to document data elements in each respective database.

---

10. https://web.stanford.edu/dept/pres-provost/cgi-bin/dg/wordpress/knowledge-nugget-business-glossary-vs-data-dictionaries/

Once that work is done, your council should confirm that the definitions for these elements are consistent across systems and store those definitions in the data dictionary. If you audit data definitions across systems and find that the same term is defined differently in one database vs. another, your data governance council will need to address this. Once your council does the work to create data standards, the next step is to uphold them across every team and system used throughout your business.

If these databases offer space for reference data, use that to your advantage as well. This feature lets you reconcile data between systems, which can help your team find missing records as you move data between systems. Since this is par for the course with big data projects, you'll want to ensure that your data governance council has documented as much reference data as possible prior to starting each respective project. Lacking this information upfront will cause delays once the project begins. Worse, it can cause consistent data quality risks. Documenting your data upfront will save you and your colleagues major headaches in the long run.

Your Next Step

This chapter asked a lot of you. You've been tasked to find an executive sponsor for your council, confirm key principles for your council to uphold, convince colleagues to serve as data stewards, define data domains per data steward, and write a data dictionary, accounting for reference data in each database where possible.

If you're feeling overwhelmed, I don't blame you. Building your data governance council will take the most time and be the hardest aspect of this work.

If you've ever bought a plot of land and built a new house on top, you know how slow the first few months can feel. It will look like nothing's getting done as time and money accrue. You might consider cutting your losses, thinking that your end goal is too ambitious and it's best to quit while you're ahead. Then, after months (if not years) of waiting, one day you visit your new home and see it all clicking into place.

As you survey the work several people poured into this project, you realize that while your home isn't done yet, you can see the bigger picture. You've learned that projects with this scope will hit inevitable roadblocks, and you'll encounter more before your home is complete. But you also know that with the foundation firmly in place, you're equipped to overcome them.

I told you in the Preface that I want you to begin this book in Los Angeles and have a plan to build data governance upon landing in New York. While this goal is true, I don't mean to imply that this is easy work. The truth is that bringing data governance to your organization will take time, patience, and the willingness to start small. Trying to do too much, too fast could cause the whole house to collapse.

So, your homework for this chapter is to pick one initial project for your data governance council to work on after you've completed all the steps in this chapter. To gain sponsorship buy-in, make sure this project aligns with your their priorities. This will give you the chance to build a scalable process for governing data projects, get stewards involved at a manageable pace, and show why governance is the most effective way to manage big data.

When choosing your data governance council's first project, consider the current appetite for data governance. Even if your organization owns a lot of data, don't assume that senior leadership sees the need for governance. Even if they do know that it's needed, the truth is that they might not be ready or willing to lead the culture change required. All isn't lost if this sounds like your business, but that does make it even more important to take an incremental approach.

Recall that your job is to manage data at scale. You're expected to lead the tools, structure, and strategy required for your colleagues to complete successful data projects. If you can prove that data governance is the most effective way to smash this goal, you will gain more buy-in from the C-suite and prospective data stewards. The best way to gain buy-in for data governance is to start small and lead one specfic data project to success. You'll learn how to do this in the next chapter.

CHAPTER 4

Write Your Data Roadmap

In early 2000, Reed Hastings wanted to sell. As Hastings and his co-founder Marc Randolph sat in Blockbuster's Dallas office, Hastings whispered that since the video rental giant was a thousand times their size, selling their startup for $50 million was in their best interest. When Blockbuster's CEO John Antioco entered the room, Hastings proposed that if Blockbuster bought their business, they could run Blockbuster.com as its online video rental arm. But when he heard how much the acquisition would cost, Antioco declined.

You know what happened next. That startup, Netflix, went public two years later and had a $238.89 billion market cap 20 years later. Blockbuster, once the world's premier video rental service, filed for bankruptcy in 2010 before shutting all corporate-owned stores four years later. Its highest market cap? $3 billion.

As the video rental industry market's former leader, Blockbuster sat on a mountain of data that it could have used to keep growing. Had leadership seen the growth in demand for online services, they had the resources to crush competitors. Instead, they had to open their own online video rental store years after Netflix started cornering that market. By then, it was too late for them to build the data-first culture that made Netflix the new leader.

When it comes to data, most organizations are more like Blockbuster than they'd care to admit. Gartner research classified 87 percent of organizations as having low maturity in BI and analytics techniques.[1] The same research found that organizations with low maturity rarely share data between IT and

---

1. https://www.gartner.com/en/newsroom/press-releases/2018-12-06-gartner-data-shows-87-percent-of-organizations-have-low-bi-and-analytics-maturity#:~:text=More%20than%2087%20percent%20of,a%20survey%20by%20Gartner%2C%20Inc

business users. They also don't link data to clear business outcomes, and bottlenecks in the central IT team often impede data model preparation.

Whether your business wants to leverage customer data to make tailored recommendations or build new machine learning models, you can't achieve any data-based goal without a plan to get there. This chapter will share how to use a data governance roadmap as the blueprint for your data-based projects and products.

You already know how essential roadmaps are. They put your product strategy to paper, defining every product against bigger goals and initiatives like the mission statements you wrote in Chapter 1 Clarify Your Company's Mission Statement, on page 2. Effective roadmaps paint a clear picture of your product's direction, mapping each feature per sprint up to key performance indicators (KPIs).

The most advanced product roadmaps invite new ideas. I once worked for a roadmap software company which offered an ideas portal. This portal helped users collect feedback for new features, then prioritize them against company goals.

Now, apply that mindset to your data governance strategy. Thus far, you've written a mission statement for how your business will use data. You've also found data stewards who will bring that mission statement to life, and formed a data governance council to ensure that all stewards work together. In this chapter, you'll learn how to write and manage all the content on a data governance roadmap to serve as a living, single source of truth for your data strategy. To begin, break this work down into distinct phases.

Assess Your Data's Current State

You can't make progress if you don't know where you stand. It's why the first step in writing your data roadmap might be the most painful: you'll need to do a complete, honest audit of how your business uses data today. Most businesses overestimate their aptitude with data, and that (lack of) aptitude affects all the ways your business uses data. Your audit will be most effective if you start with some key considerations.

To start, there's compliance with data privacy laws. Many of these laws are relatively new, from the General Data Protection Regulation (GDPR) in Europe to the California Consumer Privacy Act (CCPA) in California. Governments enacted them to protect consumer data from misuse by businesses, like selling that data to third parties. Regardless of where your business headquarters are, it's likely that these laws affect you.

For instance, GDPR limits business's abilities to collect key data about European Union (EU) citizens, such as age, location, and socioeconomic status. Under GDPR, businesses that want to use these details must inform users of their intent to do so, and how they plan to collect that data. They must also give each person the right to explicitly opt into data profiling, and they can't subject customers to automated profiling. If your business has personally identifiable data about any EU citizens, your business must comply with GDPR even if it's based elsewhere.

Compliance is one factor, but it doesn't end there. You must also understand data in the context of your data architecture. Let's revisit the case study of redesigning a database from What Are Data Stewards?, on page 14. Recall that in this case study, you must redesign the database taxonomy because it's too tough for users to find content in the database as-is. To achieve this goal, your team's data architect asks you where a certain dataset lives. She needs this information to build a data model that accurately shows how data flows from one system to the next before that data appears on the database front-end.

If she asked for this dataset, would you know where it's stored? If you don't know offhand, do you have it documented somewhere so she can reference it? Experience taught me that for many businesses, the answer is a dual no. They don't have a clue where all their data lives, nor do they have it documented. This makes it impossible to improve your data infrastructure.

Last but not least, data quality is a concern. Do the same datasets live in two separate locations? Do your colleagues automate any of their data management, or is it all manual? If your business publishes proprietary data, who cross-checks it for accuracy?

To complete an accurate data audit, you'll need to find and write down answers to several questions about data compliance, data architecture, and data quality. It helps to break them down per section, like this.

Data Compliance:

- Whom do you collect data on?
- Which type of data do you collect?
- Where do these people live?
- Which (if any) data privacy laws protect people in the geographic regions where they live?

Data Architecture:

- Where does your organization store data?
- Do these databases integrate with each other? If so, how?

- Are these storage solutions on-premise? In the cloud? Both?
- Who has access to these systems and each data domain within them?
- How are permissions granted per system, and who grants them?
- Who oversees security for these systems?

Data Quality:

- Does your organization produce unique data? If so, which colleagues manage it?

- Who cross-checks this data for quality control?

- How long does the full data production process take, from collection to dissemination?

- How (if at all) does your organization share data across departments?

- If your organization publishes data that turns out to be incorrect or non-compliant, what's your process for correction?

- Does this process apply to all aspects of data collection/sharing, or does it change per dataset or data domain?

- Which format(s) do you store data in? Does this format ever change? If so, when?

Since you're writing down answers to these questions, this is a good time to remind you how crucial documentation is for good data governance. Keep the documentation you're currently writing in an accessible space that all data stewards will use and access. When considering which documentation tool to use, start by asking which products your organization already uses.

For instance, if your technical team uses Jira to manage sprints, you can use Confluence for data governance documentation. The same parent company (Atlassian) makes both tools, which means that Jira and Confluence integrate with each other. This works in your favor by helping your data analysts, scientists, and engineers map their current tasks to your data stewards' work.

Let's say you have an epic in Jira that captures all the child issues needed to design a data model. Those child issues might include tasks like writing acceptance criteria, building Node diagrams, implementing the data model, and migrating data to your database server. You can link this epic and respective child issues in Jira to your data governance documentation in Confluence. This will give the data architects and engineers who design data models a guide to have on hand as they work.

Ideally, some of these data architects and engineers serve as stewards on your data governance council and helped write the documentation for conducting quality assessments. Using the right integrated tools gives them an easy way to link technical tasks with your data governance plan, allowing them to see how their work affects the big picture.

Thus far, you've assessed and documented how your current data governance stacks up against compliance, quality, and architecture. Now that it's on paper, the next step is to build a process map which illustrates the knowledge you've gathered.

Create a Current State Process Map

Your process map will visualize all aspects of the process you're trying to fix through your data-focused project. Done well, it's a collaborative effort amongst data stewards that breaks down silos between teams.

Breakdowns in data-sharing result from a lack of trust and transparency. It's one reason why you should have a single data governance council, rather than creating separate councils per team. When you document your current data state holistically, then share it with all members of your data governance council, you ensure that everyone has the same visibility. This will help your stewardship team write a process map that's accurate and holistic.

As your data stewardship team builds the current state process map, keep some crucial ground rules in mind. You'll note that all the work we've done thus far, from crafting your data's mission statement to building a process map, is cultural. If you don't know why and how you want your business to use data, any data-focused projects will fail to make their biggest possible impact.

On a similar note, if your colleagues worry they'll get punished for telling the truth, they won't be honest about current problems or contribute to solutions. To encourage psychological safety, the University of New Hampshire suggests using these ground rules throughout the process:[2]

- Keep an open mind to change and maintain a positive attitude.
- Leave rank at the door; one person = one voice, regardless of position.
- Everyone on the team participates.
- Stay focused.
- Don't leave in silent disagreement.
- Practice mutual respect - do not interrupt; there are no dumb questions or ideas.
- Offer honesty.
- No blame - this is a blameless environment.

---

2.   https://www.unh.edu/lean/phase-3-develop-current-state-process-map

Once you have set and shared those ground rules, this process flow map is an ideal task for your data stewards to co-own. Depending on how your organization uses data, and how many data projects your organization has in progress, your data stewards might need to make several process maps. In that case, you can divide the process maps amongst your data stewards according to their expertise and involvement with these projects.

Use the following template to create a process map for your data governance council's project, which you picked in Chapter 3, Build Your Data Governance Council, on page 27. Choose one specific process that you're trying to improve and add every step it takes to currently complete that process, no matter how small. Your goal is to show all the work needed to complete one specific process. Your end result will be the blueprint for the step that you'll take next.

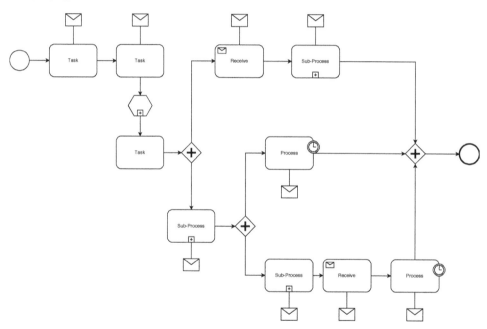

As you document each step per process, be honest above all else. While each process will have exceptions and/or desired flows, it's essential to make process maps which accurately show what really occurs. If this is nerve-racking, I understand. Even when organizations say they want to use data more effectively, they won't always do the tough, introspective work required.

If you're not cringing at your current process map, there's a good chance it isn't honest enough. And without the psychological safety established earlier, your stewards won't feel comfortable telling the truth. That derails all your efforts in the long run.

As with all templates in this book, use this process map to guide you while making one that's unique to your organization. From here, you can get more granular about which parts of the process each department owns. This is an awesome opportunity to find possible roadblocks and start solutioning for your future state. That's what you will make next.

Design Your Desired Future State for Data Governance

Once you've confirmed your data's current state, next comes the fun part: defining what you want your data's future state to look like.

When you've finished your process map(s), you'll have a baseline to make effective changes from. This will give your data stewards the chance to find opportunities for process improvement. If creativity strikes while you and your stewards build your process maps, capture those ideas in writing. Using a shared tool like Confluence works best because it lets you write down your thoughts and share them with the broader governance council. These ideas can form the basis of your data governance backlog, which allows your team to review data issues regularly.

For example, let's say you're the CTO of a nonprofit that distributes state government aid for several social services, from preschool to emergency housing. Building your process maps revealed that your nonprofit stores the same client data on several disparate servers. Most of your clients use more than one social service, yet none of your data servers integrate with each other. As a result, your organization stores client data on several servers and your social workers have no visibility into how many programs each client uses. This might cause your social workers to suggest services their clients already use, or lose track of which clients no longer need help.

In this case, you'll want to design a future state that aligns your data management against data architecture, quality, and compliance. Start by asking yourself some questions under each pillar:

Data Architecture:

- Can you consolidate data into fewer locations rather than storing it in several server/cloud environments?

- Do you rely on Excel formulas for much of your data management? If so, which tools might help you automate some of that work?

- What's a realistic timeline for moving data out of one system into another? Do you use software or database vendors that include data migration in their services?

- Are colleagues especially reliant on one software tool or database over another?

- Can you use a tool like Zapier to build integrations?

Data Quality:

- Who is in charge of managing each dataset? Is this person/team in-house or a contractor?

- Which methodologies do your colleagues use to collect and clean data?

- Have colleagues complained about specific data types, like not having the right addresses for clients? If so, which data do you notice the most problems with?

- Which format(s) is your data in? Does this format ever change?

Data Compliance:

- Who cross-checks your data for security and legal compliance? Are these compliance tasks better suited to different colleagues?

- Which compliance records do you have? Who stores these records, and where?

- If you're still mostly relying on printed paper copies, how might you move these to a secure server?

- Is client confidentiality a concern? If so, did you find occasions where data exposure might occur?

- Which colleague(s) communicate changes about data compliance to the organization? Did your process map find cases where this communication should occur more often?

As always, store your answer to these questions in the shared repository that your data governance council uses. Create separate categories per type of documentation to serve as "parent" pages that your team can quickly find. You can add "child" pages underneath each parent page which contain answers per section to these questions. If you can't answer all questions at once, you can create placeholder pages and add answers as you find them. This is an ideal task for your documentation data steward.

Once you've written these questions down, you'll need a way to know if you're on track to answer them. That involves defining what success looks like.

Choose Which Outcomes You'll Use to Measure Success

Our data-obsessed world is equally obsessed with metrics. In some ways, that's a good thing. We measure what we value, and if you're not measuring something, there's a strong chance it's not important to you.

That said, data and metrics mean nothing without context. If you notice that your social service clients drop out of your programs, it could mean that they no longer need as much consistent help. It could also mean that your clients can't confirm how to renew their memberships, learn about other programs they might use, or look up the programs they are currently enrolled in. Without conducting user research to confirm why clients slip out of your programs, you're just using data to reinforce what you want to be true.

Rather than measuring hack metrics, or selecting any metrics at all, ask yourself which outcomes you really want. Let's say that your data's mission statement includes efforts to increase client retention. You should structure your work in a way that measures specific events which represent your intended outcome. Within this context, if you notice an increase in clients searching for services from mobile devices, that alone doesn't measure success. But if your metric is to increase program sign-ups on mobile devices, you can start to confirm if your mobile experience meets this more specific goal.

Next, it's time to ask yourself which outcomes the roadmap for your future state should measure. Options might include improving practices to segment the metadata you have on your clients, migrating data from an on-premise server to cloud-based storage, auditing the data used to train your algorithms for possible bias, and upgrading data security, like enabling two-factor authentication (2FA).

2FA should be in place if it's not already, so use that option as your case study. Enabling 2FA secures your organization's data and protects it from security breaches. To achieve these outcomes, you'll need to complete a series of steps like these:

- Getting buy-in from your CEO. 2FA can't be an "IT problem." To successfully scale across the organization, senior leadership must commit to seeing it succeed. This is why sponsorship for your data governance council is so crucial.

- Confirming which enterprise systems you already use that have 2FA built in. If you use Office 365 or Google Workspace, there's a good chance you can implement 2FA via that tool's administrator permissions.

- Choosing which cloud-based product suite you'd like to scale across your enterprise for 2FA management

- Confirming which scenarios you want to enable 2FA for. You'll need to select the circumstances and frequency required to balance data security with user productivity.

- Enabling alerts for end users to receive when someone uses their credentials on a new device

- Communicating intent to use 2FA across the organization, including instructions colleagues will need to enable 2FA on their devices

Once you've confirmed the steps you'll need to hit your goal, you'll categorize steps based on effort and importance. For example, you might create a quadrant that tracks tasks against business impact and professional effort. With this in mind, try putting the previous steps into a matrix map. It will help your data governance council allot budget to tasks that will add the most value. The following matrix map gives you space to categorize steps for enabling 2FA into four separate quadrants based on proposed impact and effort.

This matrix map is a blank slate, and that's the point. It's space for you and your data stewards to sort the steps you must take into quadrants that help you separate low-impact, high-effort tasks from high-impact, low-effort tasks. Once you've finished this exercise, you'll have a list of high-impact tasks to go on your data roadmap.

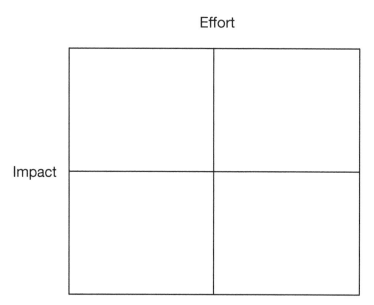

To start, write down the key criteria and considerations you'll need to make your project happen. Once you've written them all down and asked your data stewards to add theirs as well, sort the tasks in each box according to expected impact and effort. You will see boxes in each square's center reminding you how to sort cards. Once everyone's proposed tasks are in, host a meeting to review everyone's additions and prioritize the highest-impact tasks as a team. This is an ideal activity to do during a data governance council meeting when everyone is already in the same room.

Once you've acknowledged your current state of data usage and defined your desired future state, your next job is to make a plan for achieving your ideal future state. All your work in this chapter thus far primes you to write your data roadmap.

Put Prioritized Ideas on Your Data Roadmap

It's time to take all the key outcomes you want your data project to achieve, write down the steps and resources needed to achieve each goal, and assign data stewards to own each aspect of the work. Once you've confirmed each step per goal, you're ready to put it all in one roadmap.

This roadmap encompasses people, processes, and technology. Any technology needed to achieve your data goals should help your team share, store, and/or analyze data. You've chosen the data stewards involved due to their domain expertise, which will help your organization improve its data efficacy. And the processes that each data steward uses should help your team achieve each goal as fast as possible.

It's important to recall that roadmaps aren't static. Product roadmaps change as business needs and customer requirements do. Likewise, agile businesses iterate often based on clear, consistent feedback. Your data roadmap is no different. Data stewards will leave, business needs might evolve, and you'll gain more data that might influence decisions. This is all normal and necessary.

That said, your data's mission statement shouldn't change. The "how" of achieving that mission will evolve, but your reason for doing this data project shouldn't. Keep this "why" at the forefront of your roadmap, perhaps as a summary up top. Even if you've found senior sponsorship, that sponsor will ask you to present your data governance efforts to new audiences. You'll need a clear, consistent statement to frame your roadmap for new readers and make the biggest impact.

As you write the steps needed to achieve each outcome, ask yourself whom these changes will affect the most. Of course, you'll assign key tasks and outcomes to the appropriate data stewards. But you are also proposing new outcomes that will likely affect folks beyond the data governance council. If you've ever tried shepherding new software into a business, you know how hard convincing folks to adopt it can be. You also know that employee resistance to using new tools is the key reason why most new software fails to make a big business impact.

Sure, software isn't the right fit for every organization, and some tools really are a bad fit for your business. But it's also possible that while software checks every box on paper, its user interface is too confusing for your colleagues and they keep using unofficial tools to do their work rather than the new software you've tried to roll out. Left unaddressed, you might have similar problems scaling data governance throughout the org.

To avoid this, think from the outset about where resistance to this change might come from. Which groups within your org will be affected by the data governance rollout? Which colleagues do you need buy-in from, and who might be the most resistant to this work? Where will you get the budget for these data projects, and who (if anyone) must approve time for your data governance council to meet?

You don't need answers to these questions right away, but it helps to start creating solutions in tandem with your roadmap. For instance, your Chief Marketing Officer likely won't be pleased to hear that her team can't leverage data on European users due to GDPR legislation. Not using and collecting data on those users might hinder your data governance compliance, trust, and transparency requirements. It might also impede your CMO from hitting her own team goals. You can't indirectly hamper other colleagues' work and expect them to support you.

It is not your job to do your CMO's work for her, but you are responsible for writing a roadmap that proposes new, improved ways to achieve shared business outcomes. So, if the project on your data governance roadmap is a plan to encrypt data on European users, invite your CMO to give ongoing feedback as you write your roadmap.

At bare minimum, she will need to know what's coming so she can plan accordingly. In an ideal state, she will give her own feedback on this specific challenge, which you can account for in both your end solution and your roadmap itself. It's one of many benefits to having a cross-functional data governance council. When colleagues across the business own aspects of data governance, they can help define what that looks like for their own work. It also reinforces how essential data is for everyone's roles, even when they're not on the data team.

Considering these questions as you work buys you time to consider colleagues' needs and address their concerns upfront. Ideally, many of the folks whom this work will most affect serve on your data governance council. Loop them in where possible, explaining how their own work might change and co-creating new processes. At the start of your roadmap efforts, plan a weekly meeting to review progress on the roadmap and check in with each other. You can decrease this meeting cadence as the roadmap gets more mature. Until then, over-communication matters more than the alternative.

Your Next Step

As always, a chapter's end is a great place to reflect on how far you've come. Thus far, you've written your mission statement for how your organization will use data. You also selected data stewards to achieve that mission, and established your data governance council. Now that you've got a template for what a data governance roadmap does, your homework is to write a data governance roadmap for your own business.

Fill in the following template with your own data project's objectives, outcomes, and owners. Think about the data-based project you want to complete, consider the goals you must hit to do so, and assign respective stewards to lead each specific goal. To fill out this diagram, list key milestones up top with respective tasks per milestone underneath. You can use the columns on the left to denote time passed in months or quarters (grey boxes) and the metrics you're measuring (black boxes). Your roadmap's reader should broadly understand when you aim to hit each milestone, but don't lock yourself into specific dates. Those will come when you have a release plan.

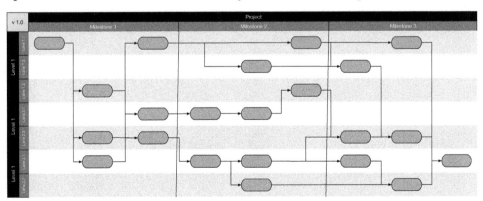

During this exercise, ask yourself, "What's the worst that could happen?" In other words, where might you take a wrong turn on the way to data maturity? Perhaps a data steward who owns customer success data freezes their technical colleagues out of key conversations. Maybe your CEO drastically shifts business priorities midway through the quarter. What if your data governance council comes to a gridlock when it's time to decide which data lake you'll need?

Imagining the worst isn't meant to scare you; it's a pragmatic way to plan for and avoid risk. From possible breaches to silo-ing the data needed for a big decision, each task on your roadmap brings its own risk to the table. You can't spot each potential risk beforehand, but you can have the foresight to see what might occur. This is part of the process to build a resilient roadmap.

Change is the only thing you can count on, and your plans to achieve good data governance will evolve with your business. Writing a data roadmap with key tasks and milestones doesn't set all your plans in stone; it does the opposite by giving you a path out of the woods when plans evolve. As long as you can answer why you're writing this roadmap, your data governance team is on the right track.

As you write your roadmap, I'm guessing that several of your goals involve development work. You might wonder what data governance looks like in development and production environments. This is the next step on your data governance journey.

CHAPTER 5

Practice Governance-Driven Development

Watching clients say they'll "get to" data governance once they've confirmed why their data projects failed inspired me to write this book. All the trendy tools in the world won't save your work if you don't have the right team and roadmap to lead it. The good news is that you're already several steps ahead of the game.

After writing your mission statement for data usage, selecting data stewards, forming a data governance council, and writing the roadmap for your council's first project, you've made the commitment to put strategy first. Now that you've laid this strong foundation, it's time to apply this work to your development process.

Contrary to common opinion, data governance isn't separate from development. It succeeds when you take time to integrate it throughout your development processes. This ensures not only that you'll make it to production, but that your data products will thrive for the long haul.

In this chapter, you'll use Zhenzhong Xu's experience scaling real-time data infrastructure at Netflix[1] as a case study to operationalize data governance.

Xu's full blog post on this subject is well worth a read, as is his talk on the subject from O'Reilly's Velocity Conference.[2] His talk and blog post both share his engineering team's full process scaling real-time data infrastructure in detail. For this chapter, you'll learn how Xu applied data governance to this problem, and played a key role helping Netflix become the streaming giant we all know and use today. You'll see how data governance principles, practices, and people show up in the development process.

---

1. https://zhenzhongxu.com/the-four-innovation-phases-of-netflixs-trillions-scale-real-time-data-infrastructure-2370938d7f01#95d1
2. https://www.oreilly.com/library/view/velocity-conference-2017/9781491976340/video314554.html

As you read each step in the case study, it will become increasingly clear how essential good governance is. You can't successfully manage data at this scale without a governance plan in place. And while Netflix might seem too different from your own organization, Xu's situation shows how data governance helps even the hardest projects succeed.

Ask if You Have the Right Data Infrastructure

2015 was a great year for Netflix. The streaming service ended Q4 that year with 4.33 million new subscribers signed up, beating analyst expectations. That growth sent the company's stock price soaring 121 percent above the prior year. Journalists noted that its content costs rose rapidly as well, from $6 billion in 2012 to $10 billion in 2015. Netflix spent more to produce content than it gained in revenue during the same period. Still, subscriber growth was so strong, especially from abroad, that its future looked bright.

The software engineering team at Netflix knew its pipelines weren't ready to meet this demand. At the time, Netflix had 500 microservices generating over 10 petabytes of data each day. This format meant that Xu's software engineering team couldn't do on-demand analytics at scale. To build the predictive analytics that would make the brand famous, Netflix needed to move its logs from the online transactional processing (OLTP) edge to an online analytics processing data warehouse (OLAP).[3]

Why? These tools support different types of data. OLTP supports row-oriented access patterns, while OLAP support column-oriented access patterns. Xu learned that if Netflix tried using OLTP to find the average session length across millions of users, its full table scans could lock the database. That would leave Netflix unavailable for users.

To complicate matters, logging volume at Netflix increased from 45 billion events per day in 2011 to 500 billion events per day in 2015. Its logging infrastructure—a mix of Chukwa, Hadoop, and Hive—wasn't built to support on-demand audience analytics, or the streaming-first solution that Netflix envisioned. At this point, Xu realized that his team had six months to successfully migrate 500 microservices worth of data to streaming-first data architecture.

While this might seem like a technical problem, it's an awesome example of data governance done well. Netflix had a clear mission for using real-time data: understanding which types of content kept its users most engaged so it could invest more in entertainment that would keep viewers enraptured.

---

3.   https://www.ibm.com/cloud/blog/olap-vs-oltp

Xu's software engineering team knew this mission when assessing whether they could achieve it with their current tech stack. They answered their own question upon learning that achieving their mission would involve migrating from logs (OLTP) to a data warehouse (OLAP). This created several action items for Xu's team:

- Research which data warehouses were the best fit for Netflix's data-specific goals.

- Ask if Netflix already had the type of warehouse they needed, or if they would need to purchase it.

- Clarify the tech procurement process at Netflix to see how long it might take to buy and implement a new warehouse.

- Write a migration plan to move 500 microservices worth of data to the new warehouse.

- Confirm if this migration could occur within the necessary timeframe.

- Write a roadmap with key tasks and milestones outlining who would own which tasks to meet the migration deadline.

- Review which data stewards would assist this effort and get buy-in from their managers.

Xu's challenge shows why it's so essential to have a data governance strategy, stewards, and council in place before starting a big project. It also illustrates why you should focus on one project at a time. Once this problem's scope became clear, Xu knew that his team had to move fast. He also realized that a goal which seemed straightforward involved a lot of moving parts and people.

That's why the first step towards data governance in development is to confirm if you have the infrastructure to achieve your mission statement. If not, your data stewardship council will need to procure it or build it from scratch, depending on your project's needs. This adds scope to your project that you'll need to account for, although your work from Chapter 4 should position you to answer it before your project kicks off.

Include Technical Partners in Your Data Governance

Netflix knew that streaming architecture would best support its end goal to ingest and analyze big data at scale. But at the time, this type of architecture was new, so using it carried some risk. What if the architecture didn't end up scaling? What if it lacked enough maintainers to address security flaws in the architecture? If Netflix chose to use it, that could jeopardize a huge amount of data.

Xu knew these risks and built a data governance plan to overcome them. Instead of abandoning the streaming architecture, his team carefully chose which partners they would use for both streaming architecture and containerization. Xu set up biweekly calls with these partners to share two-way updates, see which goals were impending, and discuss/remove blockers. While not data stewards per se, these tech partners played a key role in the governance process. In a blog post detailing the data migration, Xu explains their partnerships like this:

> Externally, we worked with partners who were leading the stream processing efforts in the industry, e.g., LinkedIn (Kafka and Samza team), Confluent, Data Artisan (builders behind Apache Flink, and later renamed to Veverica). Doing so allowed us to contribute to the OSS for our needs while leveraging the community's work.

> ...in 2015, it was still the early days of container virtualization technology. We needed a strategy to deploy quickly. Internally, we partnered up with the newly created container infrastructure Titus team. Titus was built on top of Apache Mesos and provided compute resource management, scheduling, and isolated deployment, via an abstracted API. Titus later evolved to leverage K8S in early 2020, and their team managed to migrate all workloads transparently. Thanks to this partnership, we didn't have to worry about the low-level compute infrastructure while building the data platform.

This part of the story has a key takeaway for data governance: be extremely clear about which partners are the best fit for your data efforts. This seemingly obvious goal is surprisingly hard to achieve. Tool zealots who insist that applied machine learning can only occur in PyTorch, or "fastai is just a toy," can become a real blocker. Big data's rapid rise over the last decade has yielded a range of tools to try managing it. If you start shopping for tools without knowing what your project needs to succeed, you risk choosing the wrong tech partners for your project. I say "partners" because despite what some vendors might claim, no tool can manage all aspects of big data.

Your data governance council will need to choose the right tech stack for your project and organizational data goals. This need to select data governance tools at scale makes it even more important that you choose not just the right types of tech, but the right vendors to serve as committed partners. No matter your use case, some tried and true tips apply:

• Confirm which resources you have first. You'll need to search for vendors that can help, but don't forget to look internally before searching outside your organization. For instance, let's say that you need help parsing data that's nested within thousands of PDFs. Depending on your project's budget and timeframe, you might need to hire an external vendor to parse the metadata you need from these PDFs. But before you start scheduling demos, review who's on your current team. If you have some robotic process automation (RPA) experts, you might be able to have them help you, either on a project basis or by joining your data governance council. Tempting as it is to see what's out there, don't ignore the resources you have in-house.

- Ask which job(s) you're hiring new tech to do. Let's say that you have a data lake to manage your metadata, storage, and computing power that lets you express calculations via SQL. If you lack structure and schema, a data warehouse might be a strong addition. Depending on which cloud vendor you already use, many sell data warehouses that integrate with their cloud environments. (Such as using Amazon Redshift on top of Amazon Web Services, or Google BigQuery on top of Google Cloud.) Alternatively, data warehouses like Snowflake let you use a warehouse without being tied to a proprietary cloud. Knowing which data infrastructure gaps you must fill will help you narrow down your search.

- Search for partners in open source spaces. Imagine that you review your current data stack and see that you need a novel addition. (Like Xu realizing that Netflix needed streaming architecture when this technology was new.) In that case, do your research to find tech partners with responsive maintainers and active communities. If you find a strong community leading an open source project that meets your data needs, you can offer your commercial support in exchange for contributing to and shaping the project. This allows your data stewards to help shape an upcoming open source project while including the community's work in your own.

Finding the right external partners can make all the difference for your data projects. Whether you have colleagues working beyond your data governance council or an open source community to lean on, these people can fill much-needed gaps and help bring your project to production faster. The trick is knowing which gaps you need them to fill so they can get right to work. If your project vision and roadmap are clear, finding the right partners to fulfill them is easier.

Build with a Few High-Level Customers in Mind

Xu's team at Netflix chose to pursue a streaming-first architecture so the company could support rapid user growth. Given this fact, you might expect advice telling you to test your model with the largest possible user group so you can get a representative sample size. While the researcher in me wants that to be true, it's not good governance in this case.

Consider why Netflix chose to move its entire data architecture to a streaming-first warehouse: to satisfy rapid user growth. Netflix knew demand for its services was high. In fact, it was high enough for them to try a new architecture that showed strong potential to meet their needs, but was new and immature. This choice carried several risks that the streaming-first warehouse would fail. But the reason for this migration was grounded in proven demand for Netflix services.

This case study carries several data governance lessons you can use for your own project. The first is to clarify which problem you need to solve first. If you feel the need to test your proposed data governance project with a large user group, this might be a sign that your data governance council needs to confirm if there's enough customer demand for the project itself.

It also helps your council clarify what this project aims to achieve. This advice might sound basic, but it's important to emphasize. In today's data landscape, there's strong temptation to start playing with the latest data tools "because you can." (You'll tackle that challenge later in this chapter.) In Netflix's case, they knew the best chance at long-term success with their warehouse was to test it on a few carefully selected users who could give quality feedback and evaluate the project's results during the data migration.

Netflix could proceed with user testing because they had their business case in place. When considering which folks to include for your own project, ask yourself the following questions:

- Who are the power users for your product and/or business?

- How often do you communicate with these users?

- Do these users have ongoing opportunities to give feedback? If so, how do you capture that feedback?

- Which person or team is ideal to connect with these power users and manage the product validation process?

This is an ideal subject of discussion at your next data governance council meeting. You will already have the business case for your own project documented, and a roadmap to execute the project. Once those are in place, you'll use data governance council meetings to manage the project logistics through updates and assignments.

The colleagues closest to your customers might not work on the data or IT teams. But if you have Design, Product, and/or Customer Success teams, including some colleagues as data stewards will help you find the right test users faster. For instance, having a designer serve on the council allows them to conduct user interviews and own the qualitative data from those interviews. This includes sharing the interview transcripts with other council members and storing them in your shared communications tool.

Give Your Data Stewards Room to Fail

Remember, you're in the governance-driven development stage, not the production stage. Once you've progressed to production, the time for experiments is done. Until then, use development as your sandbox to learn what does and doesn't work for your data project.

This is especially crucial if you're using new or immature tech. Managing big data demands a lot of moving parts under the hood. Xu describes this challenge when explaining how Netflix transitioned its data platform into containerized cloud infrastructure:

"There are hundreds of thousands of physical machines powering the cloud in each data center underneath the hood. At this scale, hardware failures are inevitable. When these failures arise unexpectedly, it could be challenging for the systems to keep up with the availability and consistency expectations. It's even more challenging in an unbounded low latency stream processing environment where any failure recovery can result in backpressure buildup. Cloud-native resilience for a streaming-first architecture would mean significant engineering challenges."

How did Xu surmount these engineering challenges? Instead of avoiding them, he designed the system to monitor, detect, and tolerate them. If this sounds a lot like DevOps, you're correct.

Remember when you asked yourself what's the worst that could happen while writing your roadmap in Chapter 4, Write Your Data Roadmap, on page 43? Revisit that worst case scenario now. If you are truly breaking ground with your project, I guarantee that you'll fail several times in both expected and surprising ways. Xu and his team certainly did.

On launch day at Netflix, the Kafka cluster his team built proved to be too big. Once this cluster reached its scaling limit, it couldn't recover after one of 200+ brokers died. This caused mass data loss across Netflix, even though Xu's team had correctly predicted the right amount of traffic. Thanks to the psychological safety on his team, he knew they could recover from this mishap. He also knew that this mistake was too dire to occur again.[4]

---

4.   https://kafka.apache.org/intro

Kafka streaming technology was new at the time. Although it led the stream processing architecture market, few (if any) organizations were using it at scale with the amount of data Netflix had. Using new architecture to solve a novel business challenge with big data at scale was bound to fail at some point. Xu realized that to help his team succeed, he had to give them more direct experience with Kafka so they could learn how it worked.

He did this via weekly Kafka cluster failover drills. Whoever had on-call duty each week stimulated a Kafka cluster failure. In response, the team would migrate all traffic to a different, healthy cluster without impacting users. This response is data governance in action. It gives stewards a safe, controlled environment to figure out the best tools and responses to unforeseen problems.

This might sound counterintuitive. If you're used to working on projects that use the waterfall methodology[5] (or projects that use agile in name only), you are likely more familiar with the adage that failure's not an option. If each step didn't succeed, the project writ large failed.

Perhaps most crucially, feedback in this environment doesn't come until post-production. As Alex Bunardzic explains, "We worked under the pressure that every step must be a fully qualified success. We were going out of our way to avoid getting any feedback. Feedback was reserved for the momentous Big Bang event; the point when we all got an earful on how much the system we built missed the mark. That was, in a nutshell, the traditional way of learning that we failed."[6]

You can't afford to learn this way with big data projects. Hearing that you pushed bad data to the public through production has real-world implications. People could trade on incorrect information, face undue discrimination for jobs, get their loan application denied, or receive the wrong diagnosis.

Ethical debt is technical debt. When incorrect data is found within a model, your only recourse is to scrap the model and retrain from scratch at the point where you find bad data. The best way to avoid this is to get data stewards comfortable with the tools they're using and give them space to try new techniques in development prior to production.

This gives them the hands-on training and professional freedom to gain experience that avoids problems in production. It's also a key reason why documentation plays such a crucial role in data governance: you can only give data stewards room to fail if you've given them the tools needed to do

---

5. https://www.umsl.edu/~hugheyd/is6840/waterfall.html
6. https://medium.com/@alexbunardzic/failure-is-essential-in-devops-culture-dace2a72bfa1

their work. The framework, roadmaps, and data dictionaries you've built are tools to help your stewards do their jobs, learn new skills, and keep building the business by bringing your mission statement to life.

Start Scaling Past Your Super Users

Xu's team overcame initial hurdles to ship its MVP and migrate the key customers who had participated in early user testing. Next came their toughest challenge yet: scaling that success across engineering teams at Netflix and migrating their full customer base.

They quickly confirmed that this would be a tough task. Moving past their first few MVPs put them face to face with two distinct-yet-opposing customer pain points. One user group preferred a fully managed, easy-to-use service, while the other wanted flexibility to solve more advanced business problems.

In their quest to serve both customer needs at scale, everything Xu's team touched seemed to break. Titus (their managed container infrastructure) and Spinnaker (their continuous deployment platform) lay among the carnage of trying to scale hundreds of customer deployments programmatically.

Regardless of your own toolkit, you can expect that things will go sideways in your own data project. That's why all the work you completed for your data roadmap is so essential. If you can review your roadmap with an eye on parts where work might break down, you can plan ahead to avoid or at least mitigate it. Whatever your own data project is, some strategic bets from Netflix apply:

- Choose your simplest option to start. Instead of exposing Netflix's entire complex infrastructure, Xu prioritized a highly abstract, fully managed service to meet general streaming needs. This was a crucial choice for scaling the infrastructure beyond Xu's own team across engineering at Netflix. Each team could use the data routing as a building block for their own Platform services. It also allowed users to prioritize their own needs by applying data routing to their business use cases.

- Find new opportunities for existing architecture. Can you build new product entry points on infrastructure your team already uses? If so, you're better off using that than building new products in isolation. After launching the initial Keystone product, Xu wanted to build a new platform that could harness stream processing with Apache Flink. He wanted to build a new, internal customer segment while refactoring their current architecture. By decreasing redundancies between Keystone and Flink platforms, Xu configured the Flink platform to support existing Keystone and new custom use cases. To quote Xu, "Simplicity attracts 80 percent of the use cases. Flexibility helps the bigger use cases."

Your Next Step

This chapter gave you a set of steps needed to shepherd your data through development. With Netflix as your north star, you learned the importance of using the right tools to fulfill your mission statement and how to engage tech providers as data governance partners. You found the value of building with key users in mind, then got guidance on how to scale your minimum viable product to bigger user groups.

Most importantly, you learned why it's so crucial that you give data stewards room to fail in development, and how to keep this from affecting production. Remember when you learned how to write your process map, and how essential it is that your data stewards do this in a blameless environment? Done well, that ethos carries teams into production and beyond.

As you prep your own project for development, your next step is to avoid the trap that many data governance efforts slip into: failing to integrate governance into development activities. Data governance isn't a test that you pass before getting back to data science. If you don't integrate data governance into your data projects, all the work you've done is useless.

I know it can seem like governance is abstract, and that the work you've done thus far is in lieu of your daily activities. The truth is that designing data projects to include governance avoids needing to do it later. It also helps you avoid technical debt by covering your bases at the outset.

To achieve your next step, review your own data for the project outlined in your data roadmap. Is each piece of metadata accounted for? Are relationships between data and databases defined? Does the data in your project have consistent definitions that are documented in a dictionary that everyone can access? How many data objects will you approve for reuse?

Remember that no matter what your data project is, you will need to assess data against your data governance council's pre-defined business and technical rules. The rules give your metadata meaning, turning it from raw input to actionable insights. So, before pushing to production, take time to assess the data that you are feeding your model against your data governance standards. It will ensure that the work you produce aligns with pre-defined goals that all stewards agree on. It also prepares you for the final step in this six-part process: managing data in production.

CHAPTER 6

Monitor Data in Production

I subscribe to several newsletters. In January 2022, one weekly newsletter from the author Anne Helen Petersen shared the concept of policy drift. First proposed by Jacob Hacker, policy drift describes problems that arise when policies built to serve specific social needs are not updated to solve modern problems.[1]

As one example, Section 230 is a piece of U.S. legislation that protects website platforms from being held liable for third-party content.[2] Signed in February 1996, this legislation intended to distinguish website providers from traditional publishers. Suffice to say, it fails to account for social media, big data, and a range of realities that exist today. That leaves companies like Meta largely unchecked and unregulated, which yielded scandals like the Cambridge Analytica data breach.[3] Section 230 might have met the moment when President Clinton signed it into law, but it's inadequate for today's issues.

As I read Petersen's newsletter, I saw parallels between policy drift in politics and model drift in data. It's common for machine learning teams to think that reaching production equals success. The thinking goes, "If I can just monitor my data until then, I'll know that my data governance worked."

Here's the more complex truth: if your data governance plan doesn't address data drift, it will ultimately fall short.

Data drift occurs when unexpected, undocumented changes to data structure, semantics, and infrastructure affect data quality. In machine learning, environmental changes affect how the data used to train algorithmic models

---

1. https://annehelen.substack.com/p/what-a-rugged-resilient-society-demands
2. https://crsreports.congress.gov/product/pdf/R/R46751
3. https://www.wired.com/story/cambridge-analytica-facebook-privacy-awakening/

engages each other throughout the training process.[4] Given how much data companies own today, and how much data models are exposed to throughout their life cycles, data drift is inevitable. The good news is that having models lose predictive power is far from a death sentence if teams catch data drift on time and stewards have a plan to govern data throughout each life cycle.

In this chapter, you'll explore what data governance looks like once your data project is in production. You'll see how to apply your data governance framework to the data monitoring process, from finding bottlenecks in production to ensuring that the data your models keep consuming meets quality standards. When you've finished this chapter—the last one in our book—you will have a plan in place to meet and beat data drift head-on.

The sources in this chapter expand on each subject and are ideal places to keep learning once you turn the final page. This chapter's goal is to give you the steps you must take regardless of your unique data work. No matter your project(s), you'll need life cycle plans, production monitoring, and regulation tracking to succeed. This chapter will show you how to build them.

Make a Plan to Govern Data Throughout the Life Cycle

You know from reading this book how much variance there is amongst data types, let alone data projects. So, it follows that data life cycles differ depending on context. You've set up your data governance council to manage data throughout each respective life cycle. That means it's not enough to govern data through processing and storage. You will also need a plan to govern data at key phases towards the end of each life cycle: data usage, data archiving, and data destruction.[5]

Data Usage

This stage is both the biggest opportunity and biggest risk for data governance, because this stage is where folks within and outside your organization consume your data in diverse ways. If your data team deploys analytics dashboards for your clients to use, publishing those dashboards on your company's website enables your clients to use this data for their benefit. If your datasets have unchecked problems, you'll find out in the data usage stage.

This is also the stage where you'll test if your data governance council's decisions work. Since data usage involves access needs, your data security

---

4.   https://streamsets.com/why-dataops/what-is-data-drift/#:~:text=Data%20Drift%20Defined&text=Data%20drift%20is%20unexpected%20and,new%20opportunities%20for%20data%20use.

5.   https://www.oreilly.com/library/view/data-governance-the/9781492063483/ch04.html

will be tested at this stage. If a third party audits your data for bias, it's most likely to be in this stage as well, especially if your organization sells data as its product.

Data usage shows how your organization shares data, and how people consume it. Any constraints on your council's data governance will reveal themselves at this stage.

Data Archiving

If you've ever done a data migration, then you're familiar with data archiving. It's the process of copying data from one active environment and moving it to another. Let's say you host public-facing data that your company owns within an on-premise server and want to migrate it to a cloud computing platform. Data archiving involves having data engineers manage the migration process through these steps:

- Moving your raw data from the on-premise environment into the cloud environment

- Putting this raw data into ETLs

- Cleaning this data within ETLs, then moving refined data to the dev//test database

- Connecting the test database to the API and user interface

- Turning on the data pipeline in your cloud environment so that data displays on the database front end

- Encrypting and decrypting data throughout the migration to meet data governance standards for security

If all goes well, your users shouldn't know that you've switched environments. To manage this process smoothly and efficiently, your data governance plan for data archiving should answer three key questions:

- How long will your team retain this data?
- Where will your team store this data?
- Which controls will you apply to this data?

No usage or maintenance should occur during the archive process. Once your data is in your cloud platform of choice, your team must destroy data from the archive storage.

Data Destruction

I know from experience how painful this step can be. Many organizations store any and all data that they've ever owned. I once worked on a project that required my team to automate the process of extracting data from more than 52,000 PDFs ahead of a website migration—and that 52k was post-audit, meaning there were even more beforehand.

Your business can't afford to keep all this data. Data centers and servers cost huge amounts of money and demand consistent maintenance. Beyond that, continuing to host data indefinitely yields compliance issues. That's why data destruction is an ideal task for your compliance data steward. They can clarify the data you don't need while prioritizing the data that you do need. This involves asking the following questions:

- Is your organization required to retain data for specific periods of time?

- Is all data beholden to this mandate? If not, which data can you destroy and which data must you keep?

- Where will you store the data you must keep, and which format will this data be kept in?

- Which governmental and/or industry standards is your organization required to uphold?

- How will you confirm that data destruction occurred?

To answer these questions, ask your compliance data steward to create a timeline for the data destruction plan. They are the best steward to own this task since their role requires tracking all the policies you'll need to follow, from state regulations to industry best practices. It requires answering a few key questions, which your steward can track in template format.

MIT has a template for creating data management plans that you can use.[6] While some of these questions are unique to MIT, you can apply most of them to your own data project.

You can also use DMPTool, an open source way to build bespoke data management plans.[7] DMPTool nudges you to add your project details, collaborators, research outputs, and more. The tool's "Write Plan" section asks you to answer questions about data collection, documentation, ethics, storage, and preservation.

---

6. https://libraries.mit.edu/data-management/plan/write/
7. https://dmptool.org/

Practice Data Mesh Principles

As the volume of big data keeps growing, traditional tools used to manage it can fall short. Demand for data science led many organizations to try combining their data warehouses with big data tools. The challenge is that trying to deploy data this way can cause huge backlogs, especially in large organizations. If a single team owns both the data platform and all integrations, other teams that need analytics can lose time while they wait for their results.

Even if the data team owns all infrastructure, the volume of data they work with is often larger than what many BI tools can handle. The number of data sources is often numerous as well. This makes a strong case for not having one team manage all data in one platform. Unless your organization is small, this option is bound to cause silos, backlogs, and lost productivity. Using data mesh—an architectural pattern that lets cross-functional teams manage data domains as products—can ease these risks.[8]

Not sure what a data product is? You already work with them today. If your Head of Sales keeps your company's purchase order history in a JSON file, that JSON file a data product. Your data team can automate the file upload process so that the data refreshes daily and the latest data lives in a specific location within your cloud architecture. Data products might also be published datasets that live on someone's laptop, or machine learning models that predict various costs, from shipping dates to marketing campaigns. Data products are not new inventions that your stewards must make; they're an improved way of managing the data you have now.

Zhamak Deghani founded the data mesh concept in 2019, which promotes four principles:[9]

- Data ownership is domain-specific: data mesh architecture requires data stewards who own specific data domains and lead communication about distributed data. Rather than leaving all the work of receiving, aggregating, and cleaning data to one data scientist, data stewards own this process for their respective domains. They ensure that their data is ready for use by your BI analytics tools of choice, thus preparing the clean data for use by your colleagues and customers.

- Data is a product: this is a mindset shift for many data practitioners. Rather than managing data as a service, data mesh takes a product attitude towards

---

8. https://docs.microsoft.com/en-us/azure/cloud-adoption-framework/scenarios/cloud-scale-analytics/architectures/what-is-data-mesh

9. https://www.oreilly.com/library/view/data-mesh/9781492092384/

data management. When data stewards manage their data as products, they're able to use it in more diverse ways. For instance, rather than using data about customer interactions in that single business context, you can use customer data in a range of ways that benefit your business.

• Data available as a self-service infrastructure: data mesh architecture keeps all domain data on a central platform that manages storage, streaming, pipelines, and more. This prevents data from living in disparate systems and eases the need to build integrations, APIs, and so on. It allows each data steward to manage their domain data from the same source.

• Ecosystem governance: governance is a core tenet of successful data mesh. It reinforces the framework and mission statement you wrote in Chapter 1, ensuring that all data is formatted, standardized, and discovered against equal standards. These standards give everyone the assurance that the data they use is controlled for quality.

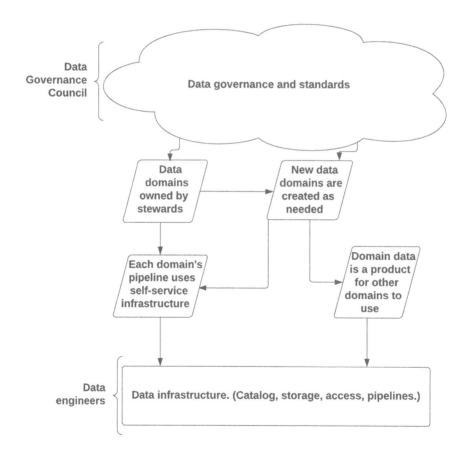

This move to distributed architecture through a shared sense of ownership is one way to execute data governance. Before you can use this architectural technique, you must have clearly defined cross-functional data domains and assign each domain to stewards who own it. You also must ensure that your data platform allows domain experts to use the tools, techniques, and dashboards that serve their audiences, without depending on just one tool or team.

While data mesh is an ideal way to practice data governance, it is not the right architecture for all teams. If your organization and technical team are small, data mesh might make your work more complex. But if your organization has independent business units, autonomous teams that work independently, and data/analytics needs across these units/teams, data mesh is worth a look.

Done well, data mesh lets teams access, develop, and manage data autonomously. It also gives your data stewardship team an easier way to keep your data secure. But there's a catch: it only works if you've done the hard work to create a data-driven culture and can automate that culture's standards.

Automate Federated Data Governance

The last section of Deghani's data mesh framework emphasizes ecosystem governance. It stresses the need to automate data governance standards throughout your data mesh architecture. Doing so ensures that your whole data ecosystem meets the data quality and compliance standards that you and your data governance council decide on.

You might wonder how data stewards should manage their domains' data as unique products. Doesn't that contradict the need to standardize data? In fact, data stewards need consistent standards that guide them towards self-service data products. Policies on data compliance, ethics, security, and documentation help data stewards find, interpret, and use data to fulfill their goals. Likewise, stewards can't build and start managing their data products without knowing which tools to use, and being assured that their colleagues use these tools as well.

To ensure that your data project lives on through production, your data governance council should have a set of standards that define rules for your data mesh. These rules explain how data stewards should build their own respective data products, which are often published datasets that other domain stewards can access through data mesh. Federated data governance policies should focus on four factors:

- Interoperability, which defines the parameters that allow stewards to leverage data products across the data mesh. For example, a federated governance policy on interoperability could state that stewards should share data products as CSV files on AWS S3 in buckets owned by each respective domain data steward.[10]

- Documentation, which helps everyone learn how to find and use data products. If your team uses wikis to capture information, you can write a page which shares metadata per product. This might be the data product, URL that's hyperlinked to its location, and descriptions of each CSV field. Keeping this format simple and consistent helps everyone find the data they need and get familiar with its format.

- Security, which involves setting role-based access by creating identity and access management policies within your cloud platform.

- Compliance, which automates data requirements for everything from legal rights to personally identifiable information within your data mesh.

Federated data governance is twofold: data stewards define which standards all teams that offer data products must use. Then, your data platform automates those standards throughout your architecture. Each team that offers domain data products owns fulfillment and adherence to these standards, from each product's ideation stage through production. This keeps everyone accountable for data quality.

Execute Data Security Standards

Successful data governance efforts don't manage risk separate from engineering. Recall that when explaining their seven-step data governance framework, Gartner notes that businesses must include security risk when evaluating outcomes. Like data governance itself, your council can't tack on risk and security as afterthoughts. Instead, your council should weigh relevant risks and opportunities when defining your ideal future state, then monitor data against those standards in production.

---

10. https://www.datamesh-architecture.com/

Remember the mission statement you wrote for data use in Clarify Your Company's Mission Statement, on page 2? Your data governance council must do the same for security. This statement should be a clear, concise sentence which states how your organization commits to data security at all stages of each project. It's best for your security data steward to write this statement, with input from you to ensure that it captures organizational goals and aligns with your data mission statement. A strong data security policy must state these three things:

- Your organization's key security need
- The circumstances under which your organization must meet this need
- Operating standards which are crucial to meet this need

As always, specifics will differ depending on your business. One organization's data security policy will be different than another's depending on both organizations' needs and standards. If your own organization's key security need is confidentiality, then you'll need to ensure that all actions, standards, procedures, and circumstances meet this requirement. This directly impacts how you'll govern data in production. For instance, if you want to train an algorithm using patient data, you'll need to ensure that you use tools and techniques which mask personally identifiable information (PII).

Your data security policy thus informs every action you and your data stewards will take, from evaluating vendors based on this statement to using the right algorithmic training techniques. By the time your data project hits development, your team of data architects, engineers, scientists, and analysts should know which security standards govern their work. This ensures alignment between stewardship groups by giving security a well-deserved seat at the table early.

Include your security data steward(s) in strategic project planning, then keep them involved through the production process. It's crucial to involve security stewards as early in your process as possible. Remember in Chapter 4 when you wrote your process map for how things work today? It's best to include your security steward in those efforts so they can explain how security works as-is and share security restrictions/requirements that might impact production. This allows stewards to advise on what's possible, get buy-in from the right stakeholders, and ensure that your team has the resources to fulfill security standards at the right times, from deployment through production.

Gather security requirements early. Requirements gathering for security isn't the same as gathering business requirements. Capturing these requirements is complex, comprehensive, and can take time. It's best to start security requirements gathering as early in the process as possible, well before beginning a data migration or deploying data to production. That way, the data team in charge of your production environment knows which security standards to uphold.

Security requirements broadly fall within three categories:[11]

- Confidentiality: controlling who gets to read information
- Integrity: ensuring that information and programs are changed only in a specified, authorized manner
- Availability: confirming that authorized users have continued access to information and resources

It helps to track these security requirements using a security requirements traceability matrix (SRTM). This matrix shows security requirements, their implementation schedule, and essential resources you'll need to succeed. The SRTM is a useful tool for your security steward to own and maintain as your project's work progresses. It should show test cases, test runs, test results, bugs, and defect resolution status.[12]

Depending on your project, you'll add case-specific best practices as well. If you're managing a database, you'll add tasks like segregating data from the same server as your website, implementing HTTPS for website encryption, generating backups, implementing firewalls, and deploying full-stack observability systems.

Security includes managing metadata throughout production. Your data team will need to track metrics that include data sharing, usage, and permissions per dataset. Alongside the SRTM, your security data steward can use the data catalog your council created to track which metadata you can use for which purposes. Metadata management is a crucial yet often overlooked part of data governance. It's treated as additional information that exists outside the data at hand.

The truth is that when managed as a strategic asset, metadata boosts security in key ways. Cataloging metadata keeps it in one place where it's less likely to go missing or exist on several servers. It also ties usage restrictions and data licensing to specific data, which creates data ownership records. From a security standpoint, metadata cataloging creates records for data usage, access, and updates.

---

11. https://nap.nationalacademies.org/read/1581/chapter/4
12. https://oasas.ny.gov/system/files/documents/2022/04/requirements_traceability_matrix.pdf

When your data governance council manages metadata through production, you boost transparency and trust in your company's data. In turn, one part of your data framework (risk and security) impacts another (trust and transparency). This symbiosis helps all data stewards work towards the same goals, before and during production.

Set Specific Goals for Your Production Monitoring

All the work you've done thus far, from finding your framework for data governance to writing your roadmap, aims to democratize data by building scalable ways to manage it across your organization. You achieve this by embedding the standards you've set into your data pipelines and production processes. That way, you can automate your data governance standards and uphold these standards once your models reach production.

Thanks to the data framework you started using in Chapter One, you already know which standards you're using to measure data governance success. Now that your first data project is in production, it's time to put that framework into engineering practice.

Microsoft's blog post, "Creating a modern data governance strategy to accelerate digital transformation," gives a great overview of how they achieved this.[13] Given their product suite, they embed their own data governance standards into Microsoft tools, specifically its Azure cloud computing platform and its Visual Studio development environment.[14]

You (of course) aren't obligated to choose Microsoft for your data management. There are many products that help companies govern data, and multiple cloud computing platforms. That said, Microsoft's industry influence and big product suite make it a key player in the data governance space. Whichever option you choose, remember that tools matter less than implementing your governance framework into the right tools for your business. Here is an example of how Microsoft did it.

To start, Microsoft invested in creating data standards upfront. They formalized their governance standards as you've done throughout this book. Once those standards were written down and shared, Microsoft's data stewards set compliance measurements against these standards. Then, the stewardship team embedded these compliance standards throughout their development environment, which in their case is a single enterprise data lake platform.

---

13. https://www.microsoft.com/en-us/insidetrack/driving-effective-data-governance-for-improved-quality-and-analytics

14. https://www.microsoft.com/en-us/insidetrack/driving-effective-data-governance-for-improved-quality-and-analytics

To track compliance with governance standards, Microsoft automated its review process. They have Azure generate, assign, and track data governance standards within its data lake. When the engineering team meets certain milestones, the data steward who owns the data at hand gives a governance assessment. They review the controls, scanning, measurement, and access controls by asking a few key questions:

- Which redundant/outdated data exists?
- Who has access to this data?
- How are the stewards with access to this data using it?

By this time, your data governance council should have selected an enterprise data lake (EDL) where you can move data from disparate sources into a single source of truth. Using an EDL for your data governance efforts has two key benefits.

First, it consolidates your data in one place that all data stewards can access. When all stewards know where data exists, along with how to contribute and find the data they need, far fewer questions exist about where data lives and how to access it. EDLs also solve the constant question of where data lives and originates. It's too common for crucial company data to live in an Excel sheet on someone's local machine. If a data steward needs to track that data's origin, finding it often yields a wild goose chase. Putting all the data your company uses into an EDL saves valuable time.

Secondly, it gives your stewards a single source to do data scanning. I think we've all worked with organizations that stored data across countless systems and databases. In chaotic dev environments like these, data governance gets drastically harder. EDLs give your team a single space to view and govern data across each project's life cycle. In turn, this infrastructure helps prevent data drift.

Despite their benefits, EDLs only work if the data within them is clean and accounted for. To see how different teams use the same data, you'll need to set up lineage tracking.

Use Data Lineage Tracking

Data lineage plays a key role in your plan to embed data governance into engineering. It confirms where the data comes from, recording the path it takes over time and visualizing its flow from one system to the next. In most organizations, the same data spans several projects and pipelines. Data lineage helps data scientists track errors and find those errors' root causes. This plays a key role in your data governance, especially when it comes to fulfilling transparency and bias reduction.

For instance, let's say that your data team built an algorithm which intends to help HR review resumes for C-level roles. Post-deployment, your HR director tells the governance council that she isn't receiving applications from women. She wants to confirm if the algorithm is screening out women for these roles, preventing applications from review by a person.

To investigate, the data team that built and deployed this algorithm does a data lineage assessment. Upon reviewing the algorithm's data sources, they learn that due to indirect bias—a byproduct of sensitive attributes like gender that correlate with non-sensitive attributes like zip codes—the algorithm associates C-level leaders with men. As a result, the algorithm downgrades applications from women since women have historically not held these roles as often as men due to a range of sociocultural factors.

This is where data lineage plays a key role reducing technical debt. When your colleagues or customers find algorithmic bias, the solution is to roll back the algorithm prior to the first time your team found bias. Then, you must restart the data training process. Automating data lineage in the EDL helps your data team catch issues like this as they arise. If your team automates the data lineage process, you can decrease the need for colleagues and customers to find problems after the fact.

Successful lineage tracking depends largely on your metadata management. You'll need metadata parameters defined and your team of stewards who commit to updating metadata for their own data domains. This will help you define the amount of metadata needed to account for data lineage tracking, along with the type of lineage tracking you need. End-to-end data lineage shows a complete audit of how specific metadata is used in diverse contexts, from its input as a source to its final use cases. Your data stewards can also use a vertical view of data lineage to see the data at a more granular level.

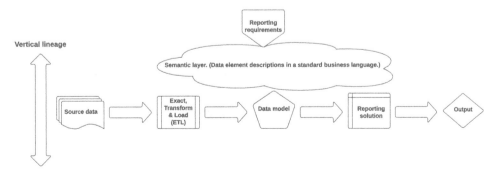

This helps teams find discrepancies with data and catch them before they reach the analytics processing stage. Let's go back to our hiring algorithm example. Had the data team used a vertical view of the data used to train this algorithm, they could have found that the data used to train it displayed indirect bias against women. That would have allowed them to spot the problem early and retrain their model pre-launch.

Data lineage helps teams find root errors in reports, comply with data privacy laws, migrate systems effectively, and more. Just like it's dependent on strong metadata management, other techniques rely on strong data lineage. Feature stores are one example of data lineage tracking in action.

Use Feature Stores to Prevent Data Drift

If you're using data to train machine learning models, you can use a feature store to catalog all available features. It gives data scientists a single place to find the raw data they need to transform it into features their machine learning models can use.[15] These features can be offline and calculated as part of a batch job (aka average monthly spend) or online and essential to calculate in real-time (such as fraud detection). Frameworks like SQL underpin offline features, whereas tracking online data demands platforms like Kafka that can track it in real time.

No matter which type of tracking you need, feature stores give data teams a single place to go where they can find the data and metadata they need per machine learning project. They also track data lineage per feature by showing how each feature was generated, then used throughout diverse data projects. Rather than manually tracking how your data teams used each feature, you and your data stewards can use feature stores to answer questions about compliance, accuracy, use cases, and more.

If you're working on this type of data project, try running this command from Adi Hirschtein, VP of Product at Iguazio. Running it can save your engineers hours of writing code:

```
df = feature_store.get("transaction_volume").filter_by (transaction_id)
```

Your data team can also verify your models by training them on data generated at least six months ago and then comparing outcomes to models trained on current data. Comparing results helps confirm if data drift occurred. Likewise, you can build a data pipeline with features that account for quality

---

15. https://towardsdatascience.com/what-are-feature-stores-and-why-are-they-critical-for-scaling-data-science-3f9156f7ab4

expectations, then correct verification errors by updating part of the data pipeline.

Srikanth Machiraju, a cloud solution architect at Microsoft, wrote an excellent overview of how to find data drift.[16] The steps that he outlines in this post share more details about how you can configure your environment to search for data drift and catch drift before it spreads.

Read this post, then set up the steps he outlines in your own production environment. Given Machiraju's role at Microsoft, this post is Azure-centric. For your purposes, the tool matters less than the techniques. You must track data lineage and prevent data drift no matter which tools you use or projects you work on.

Feature stores aren't the only way to track data in one place. Shipping data as deployable units is another technique to ingest new data at scale.

Ship New Data as Deployable Units

A large part of working with data involves building systems that can consistently ingest new data and hold it to your governance standards. You'll need to ensure that new data in your pipelines meets security standards, has its lineage tracked, meets your data governance council's quality standards, and is mapped to your data catalog. Your data governance work never ends; it scales to meet evolving needs.

For instance, let's say your job involves creating monthly reports which share data on commodity production in Texas and Oklahoma. Your colleague—the statistician who produces these reports—receives the latest data from their field office on the first Friday of each month. Adding this data to your system involves the following steps:

- Adding a new data table
- Updating your data model
- Including the new data in your catalog

You can automate those steps through the governance you've set up. Once your data project is in the development stage, governance activities start working as code. Any changes you make to your data pipelines go through your continuous deployment process, which supports automated pipeline updates. This process updates all three of these actions at the same time, so

---

16. https://towardsdatascience.com/why-data-drift-detection-is-important-and-how-do-you-automate-it-in-5-simple-steps-96d611095d93

when one of your data stewards adds these changes at the same time, your system deploys new data to production as its own unit.[17]

Viewing this ingestion process through the deployable unit lens decreases the risk that your colleagues will de-prioritize data catalog updates. This reduces your risk of issues with data quality, security, and so on. With that in mind, here's what the process described looks like when deploying new data as a unit in your pipeline.

Recall that at this stage, you're assessing new data against pre-defined data governance standards. This chart emphasizes how crucial it is to make these changes at the data catalog level. Those changes, which your statistician publishes in their next report, trigger updates to your model along with a new schema. In turn, your team deploys new data to production with assurance that it passed the data governance standards your team built.

If this process looks manual, don't fret. You've finished a lot of hard work throughout this book to set up your first data governance standards. I'm guessing this work felt manual, even arduous. The good news is that once it's done, you can automate it. Once you've built production pipelines that support and measure your governance efforts, not only do these pipelines execute the standards that your data governance council built; they also help your team improve governance by gaining new insights.

For instance, the process of ingesting new data assets offers the chance to make new categories in your data catalog, update metadata tags, assign new data to stewards, and more.[18] In order for this to work, you'll need to clarify which data you're governing, who is responsible for it, and how your data governance council measures success. Against these benchmarks, ask yourself: is all of the new data you receive secure, transparent, and up to your organization's quality standards?

17. https://medium.com/data-ops/governance-as-code-6b1e26c81f25

18. https://tdan.com/steps-to-continuous-data-governance-improvement/29208#

All the work you've done throughout this book equips you to answer that question with confidence. Once you're in the production stage with data, you can automate your framework's implementation. That is how to execute successful data governance: turn your policies into deployable units that you automate in your EDL. The more knowledge and experience you gain, the more you can improve your data governance over time. That's a must since you will need to stay on top of regulation changes, and reflect those changes in production.

Track Regulation Changes

The days of free data harvesting are done. Regulators and consumers alike have far less tolerance for companies treating consumer data as a free-for-all.[19] This is doubly true for data that has personally identifiable information, like social security numbers. As more legislation like GDPR in Europe and CCPA in California comes to pass, your business can't continue managing data like it did before, especially if you work in a highly regulated industry.

How does this impact your data governance? Your data stewardship council will need to not just track regulation changes that affect your business, but also to embed them throughout your workflows. This affects everything from how your colleagues collect data to which anonymizing techniques you might use when training algorithms. The complexity involved is another reason why it's so crucial to manage your data in a single EDL: you can see all your data at once and clarify which data is subject to new or upcoming regulations.

As of January 1, 2023, the Virginia Data Consumer Protection Act (VDCPA) applies to all people who conduct business in Virginia "and either (i) control or process personal data of at least 100,000 consumers or (ii) derive over 50 percent of gross revenue from the sale of personal data and control or process personal data of at least 25,000 consumers."[20] This bill gives consumers the right "to access, correct, delete, obtain a copy of personal data, and to opt out of the processing of personal data for the purposes of targeted advertising."

Now, let's say you're the Chief Technology Officer of a midsize bank based in McLean, Virginia. Your in-house legal counsel informs you of this impending regulation, and how your business must comply once the law goes into effect.

---

19. https://hbr.org/2022/02/the-new-rules-of-data-privacy
20. https://lis.virginia.gov/cgi-bin/legp604.exe?211+sum+SB1392

How does this impact your data pipeline? You will need to start by knowing these things:

- Which data you have
- Where it's stored
- Which products it's used for and which techniques are used to train it
- How long you retain it for
- When and how to destroy it

I saved tracking regulations for last because doing this well depends on a mature data governance program. You'll have no clue if you are meeting regulations if you don't know which data you own, where it's stored, or how it's used. That's why your data catalog and EDL techniques—including processes to use, archive, and destroy data—confirm regulation compliance.

Within your EDL, assign your compliance data steward the role of auditing data in the system against new regulations. While this steward doesn't need to be a data practitioner, they should be able to see how relevant data flows between systems and find issues in data lineage.

As part of the Virginia bank example, you might wonder how to program that accountability into your data work. Your compliance data steward could give your data engineers the parameters for a script that scans the EDL for compliance against VDCPA. Your data engineers would then implement that script and run consistent scans to ensure that all new and current data meets VDCPA standards.

This puts your business in a strong position if you're audited and/or a customer asks which personal data you have about them. It builds trust and transparency by proving that you govern data in ethical ways.

Your Next Step

Look at all that you've achieved throughout this book. When you first picked it up, you knew you needed a data governance plan and had to start from scratch. In six short chapters, you've found a framework that you'll use to govern your data, selected the right data stewards to execute this plan, built a data governance council, written a roadmap to execute your first data governance project, applied data governance to your development process, and learned how you can automate governance throughout production.

In this book's Preface, I said my goal was for you to pick this book up on a plane leaving Los Angeles and have a data governance plan once you landed in New York. While that goal stayed the same, I didn't mean to imply that data governance work is fast or easy. On the contrary, I want to acknowledge how hard, even thankless, it can feel.

There's a reason why most organizations don't have data governance: doing it well, and doing it right, takes more patience than many leaders have. Adding governance to data projects can cause those projects to stay in development longer, or to find compliance issues in production. With so many hardships already on the table, why expose even more risks, especially once you've deployed your models?

I hope the answer is already clear: you can't afford to look the other way. If you work in a highly regulated industry like finance, U.S. law already requires you to govern data. As I write this, countless cities, companies, and people are suing tech giants like Meta for data misuse. And this is in the United States, where citizens have far fewer data privacy rights than in other countries. If you work in Europe, failing to give a customer the data you've collected on them could cost you 6 percent of your annual revenue.

Governance fails when it's manual and siloed. There is too much data produced today for one person, team, or machine to manage it all. Engaging your cross-functional colleagues to co-own and manage data, from choosing which tools you'll use to finding feature stores in production, is the right way forward.

That doesn't mean throwing your marketing director into the production environment. It means your marketing director has the power to own and make decisions about the data in their department—how it's used, who can access it, when to protect personally identifiable information, and which definitions to use.

Throughout my years as a service designer, I've learned that people are much more likely to embrace solutions that they co-create. If your cross-functional colleagues have more control over their data, and are rewarded for helping your team govern it, they will be far more likely to help.

With all the tools you need to move forward, your last task (for now) is to do a data lineage assessment on the data in one of your pipelines. The specifics will depend on which tools you're using. Doing data lineage in SQL will differ than if you're using the ETL process. Regardless of your toolkit, this task will require several key steps:

- Review the key reason why this data's being used. Remember the mission statement you wrote for data use? Apply that big picture thinking to this process as well. The answer will affect the following steps.

- Confirm which department(s) the data came from, and which steward(s) own it.

- Query your EDL to find the data you're searching for within your data catalog.

- Clarify which systems this data is in and which transformation functions you have used. Is your test environment different than the production environment? If so, how does data flow between these systems, and who owns it?

- Ask if data quality changed throughout lineage hops. If so, how does this data meet compliance standards (or not)?

If you're unsure where to start, revisit the roadmap you wrote back in Chapter 4. If you're completing each chapter's next step in sequential order to finish one data project, you can apply the previous steps to your project at hand. The tool you're using to manage data at scale should have lineage visualization, which lets data stewards view how data moves from its source to final reports. Tools like Collibra also let you filter down to view data at the table, column, and query levels by clicking in to see the data as code. This step is crucial since it lets you view possible risk, such as conditional statements which might affect the final results.

No matter which project you start or which tools you use, I hope you put this book down with the confidence to lead data governance. It's true that data governance is work, but you're not meant to do that work alone. When you share data governance across your organization, write a roadmap to track progress towards achieving your mission statement, and automate data quality standards, you are on your way to mastering the art of data governance. I can't wait to see what you'll achieve.

Thank you!

We hope you enjoyed this book and that you're already thinking about what you want to learn next. To help make that decision easier, we're offering you this gift.

Head on over to https://pragprog.com right now, and use the coupon code BUYANOTHER2023 to save 30% on your next ebook. Offer is void where prohibited or restricted. This offer does not apply to any edition of the *The Pragmatic Programmer* ebook.

And if you'd like to share your own expertise with the world, why not propose a writing idea to us? After all, many of our best authors started off as our readers, just like you. With up to a 50% royalty, world-class editorial services, and a name you trust, there's nothing to lose. Visit https://pragprog.com/become-an-author/ today to learn more and to get started.

We thank you for your continued support, and we hope to hear from you again soon!

The Pragmatic Bookshelf

SAVE 30%!
Use coupon code
BUYANOTHER2023

Concurrent Data Processing in Elixir

Learn different ways of writing concurrent code in Elixir and increase your application's performance, without sacrificing scalability or fault-tolerance. Most projects benefit from running background tasks and processing data concurrently, but the world of OTP and various libraries can be challenging. Which Supervisor and what strategy to use? What about GenServer? Maybe you need back-pressure, but is GenStage, Flow, or Broadway a better choice? You will learn everything you need to know to answer these questions, start building highly concurrent applications in no time, and write code that's not only fast, but also resilient to errors and easy to scale.

Svilen Gospodinov
(174 pages) ISBN: 9781680508192. $39.95
https://pragprog.com/book/sgdpelixir

Data Science Essentials in Python

Go from messy, unstructured artifacts stored in SQL and NoSQL databases to a neat, well-organized dataset with this quick reference for the busy data scientist. Understand text mining, machine learning, and network analysis; process numeric data with the NumPy and Pandas modules; describe and analyze data using statistical and network-theoretical methods; and see actual examples of data analysis at work. This one-stop solution covers the essential data science you need in Python.

Dmitry Zinoviev
(224 pages) ISBN: 9781680501841. $29
https://pragprog.com/book/dzpyds

Exploring Graphs with Elixir

Data is everywhere—it's just not very well connected, which makes it super hard to relate dataset to dataset. Using graphs as the underlying glue, you can readily join data together and create navigation paths across diverse sets of data. Add Elixir, with its awesome power of concurrency, and you'll soon be mastering data networks. Learn how different graph models can be accessed and used from within Elixir and how you can build a robust semantics overlay on top of graph data structures. We'll start from the basics and examine the main graph paradigms. Get ready to embrace the world of connected data!

Tony Hammond
(294 pages) ISBN: 9781680508406. $47.95
https://pragprog.com/book/thgraphs

SQL Antipatterns, Volume 1

SQL is the ubiquitous language for software developers working with structured data. Most developers who rely on SQL are experts in their favorite language (such as Java, Python, or Go), but they're not experts in SQL. They often depend on antipatterns—-solutions that look right but become increasingly painful to work with as you uncover their hidden costs. Learn to identify and avoid many of these common blunders. Refactor an inherited nightmare into a data model that really works. Updated for the current versions of MySQL and Python, this new edition adds a dozen brand new mini-antipatterns for quick wins.

Bill Karwin
(378 pages) ISBN: 9781680508987. $47.95
https://pragprog.com/book/bksap1

Modern Front-End Development for Rails, Second Edition

Improve the user experience for your Rails app with rich, engaging client-side interactions. Learn to use the Rails 7 tools and simplify the complex JavaScript ecosystem. It's easier than ever to build user interactions with Hotwire, Turbo, and Stimulus. You can add great front-end flair without much extra complication. Use React to build a more complex set of client-side features. Structure your code for different levels of client-side needs with these powerful options. Add to your toolkit today!

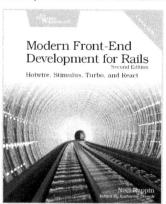

Noel Rappin

(408 pages) ISBN: 9781680509618. $55.95

https://pragprog.com/book/nrclient2

Build a Binary Clock with Elixir and Nerves

Want to get better at coding Elixir? Write a hardware project with Nerves. As you build this binary clock, you'll build in resiliency using OTP, the same libraries powering many commercial phone switches. You'll attack complexity the way the experts do, using a layered approach. You'll sharpen your debugging skills by taking small, easily verified steps toward your goal. When you're done, you'll have a working binary clock and a good appreciation of the work that goes into a hardware system. You'll also be able to apply that understanding to every new line of Elixir you write.

Frank Hunleth and Bruce A. Tate

(106 pages) ISBN: 9781680509236. $29.95

https://pragprog.com/book/thnerves

Program Management for Open Source Projects

Every organization develops a bureaucracy, and open source projects are no exception. When your structure is intentional and serves the project, it can lead to a successful and predictable conclusion. But project management alone won't get you there. Take the next step to full program management. Become an expert at facilitating communication between teams, managing schedules and project lifecycle, coordinating a process for changes, and keeping meetings productive. Make decisions that get buy-in from all concerned. Learn how to guide your community-driven open source project with just the right amount of structure.

Ben Cotton
(190 pages) ISBN: 9781680509243. $35.95
https://pragprog.com/book/bcosp

Build Talking Apps for Alexa

Voice recognition is here at last. Alexa and other voice assistants have now become widespread and main-stream. Is your app ready for voice interaction? Learn how to develop your own voice applications for Amazon Alexa. Start with techniques for building conversational user interfaces and dialog management. Integrate with existing applications and visual interfaces to complement voice-first applications. The future of human-computer interaction is voice, and we'll help you get ready for it.

Craig Walls
(388 pages) ISBN: 9781680507256. $47.95
https://pragprog.com/book/cwalexa

The Pragmatic Bookshelf

The Pragmatic Bookshelf features books written by professional developers for professional developers. The titles continue the well-known Pragmatic Programmer style and continue to garner awards and rave reviews. As development gets more and more difficult, the Pragmatic Programmers will be there with more titles and products to help you stay on top of your game.

Visit Us Online

This Book's Home Page
https://pragprog.com/book/lmmlops
Source code from this book, errata, and other resources. Come give us feedback, too!

Keep Up-to-Date
https://pragprog.com
Join our announcement mailing list (low volume) or follow us on Twitter @pragprog for new titles, sales, coupons, hot tips, and more.

New and Noteworthy
https://pragprog.com/news
Check out the latest Pragmatic developments, new titles, and other offerings.

Save on the ebook

Save on the ebook versions of this title. Owning the paper version of this book entitles you to purchase the electronic versions at a terrific discount.

PDFs are great for carrying around on your laptop—they are hyperlinked, have color, and are fully searchable. Most titles are also available for the iPhone and iPod touch, Amazon Kindle, and other popular e-book readers.

Send a copy of your receipt to support@pragprog.com and we'll provide you with a discount coupon.

Contact Us

Online Orders:	*https://pragprog.com/catalog*
Customer Service:	*support@pragprog.com*
International Rights:	*translations@pragprog.com*
Academic Use:	*academic@pragprog.com*
Write for Us:	*http://write-for-us.pragprog.com*
Or Call:	+1 800-699-7764

Ingram Content Group UK Ltd.
Milton Keynes UK
UKHW030025110323
418393UK00007B/11